P

_____

Alison

By

_____

John & Pat

On the Occasion of

_____

your Confirmation

Date

_____

15 July 2007

wishing you much
happiness in Gods love.

x x x

THE BIBLE'S GREATEST STORIES IN A YEAR

THE BIBLE'S GREATEST STORIES IN A YEAR

DANIEL PARTNER

BARBOUR
PUBLISHING

© 2006 by Barbour Publishing, Inc.

ISBN 1-59789-401-X

Previously published as *365 Read-Aloud Bedtime Bible Stories*.

Cover image © PhotoDisc

Published by Barbour Publishing, Inc., P.O. Box 719, Uhrichsville, Ohio 44683, www.barbourbooks.com

Our mission is to publish and distribute inspirational products offering exceptional value and biblical encouragement to the masses.

 Member of the
Evangelical Christian
Publishers Association

Printed in the United States of America.
5 4 3 2 1

A NOTE TO READERS

You're about to embark on a journey of discovery—a discovery of the greatest stories in the Bible. For each day of an entire year, this book provides a carefully retold account of an important biblical passage. *The Bible's Greatest Stories in a Year* offers an excellent overview of the people, places, and events that started Christian history on its world-changing way.

The text is fascinating, the language simple and clear. In fact, this volume is an adult version of an illustrated children's book entitled *365 Read-Aloud Bedtime Bible Stories*. With sales of well over two million copies, that book has generated a lot of feedback—and over the years, Barbour Publishing has received many letters from parents who said they bought the book for their children but ended up learning much about the Bible themselves. Due in part to their requests, we now provide this "adult-sized" edition—minus the kid-friendly illustrations and discussion questions—for your reading pleasure.

The stories are arranged in a chronological, as opposed to biblical, order to give you a feel for the flow of history. Each day's reading also includes the appropriate scripture references, in case you'd like to follow up with a time of Bible reading.

We hope that will be the case, and that *The Bible's Greatest Stories in a Year* will encourage you to spend more time with one of God's greatest gifts to the world: His Word. Enjoy!

THE EDITORS

DAY 1
GOD CREATES THE EARTH
PART ONE

The earth is very old. No one knows when it was made. But God has always been alive. He created the heavens and the earth. The earth was empty and very dark and covered with water. Nothing lived on the earth.

God said, "Let there be light," and there was light. God saw that the light was good. He called the light Day and the darkness Night. This was the first day. On the second day, God spoke and made the sky.

Next God said, "I want the dry land to come out of the water." So it did. God named the land Earth and the waters Sea. God saw that this was good. Then God said, "Let all the green plants grow out of the earth." All this happened on the third day, and it was good.

Then on the fourth day, God spoke again. He said, "Let the sun and moon and stars come into the sky." So this happened. God put them in the sky to give light to the earth. The sun shines in the day. The moon and stars shine at night. God saw that this was good, too.

Find It in the Bible
GENESIS 1:1–19

DAY 2
GOD CREATES THE EARTH
PART TWO

On the fifth day, God spoke again. He said, "I want the seas to be filled with living things. I want birds to fly in the sky." So God created everything that lives in the sea and flies in the sky. And God blessed them.

Then God said, "Let the animals live on earth." So he created big animals and little things that creep on the ground. God saw that all this was good.

Finally God said, "Now I am going to make human beings. Unlike the animals, they will stand up tall and have a soul. They will be like me, rule the earth, and care for it." So God took some dust from the ground and formed man. He breathed the breath of life into him. Man became alive.

God blessed them saying, "I want you to live all over the earth." God saw that everything he had made was very good. This ended the sixth day.

On the seventh day, God rested. His work was done. So He blessed that day and made it holy.

Find It in the Bible
GENESIS 1:20–2:3

DAY 3
ADAM LIVES IN THE GARDEN

The man God created was named Adam. God planted a garden in Eden to be Adam's home. This garden was big. Four rivers ran through it. Beautiful plants and trees grew there. They were good for food. God told Adam to take care of the garden.

Next God created the animals and birds out of the dust. He brought them to the man and Adam named them all. But Adam was alone. "This is not good," God said. "I will make someone to be with Adam and to help him." So God made Eve.

Find It in the Bible
GENESIS 2:8–24

DAY 4
EVE IS TRICKED BY THE SERPENT

God made Eve in a wonderful way: When Adam was asleep, God took a rib out of him. God made a woman with that rib and brought her to Adam. They loved each other. Adam named the woman Eve. They lived at peace in their beautiful garden. They cared for it as God asked, and God walked with them there.

Two special trees grew in Eden. One was named the Tree of Life. God warned them about the other tree. It was the Tree of the Knowledge of Good and Evil. "If you eat of this tree," he said, "you will die."

Now there was a sneaky creature in the garden—the serpent. He said to Eve, "Did God say you shouldn't eat of the Tree of Knowledge?" Eve answered, "He said if we do we will die."

"That is not true," the serpent lied. "Eat of it and you will be like God." Eve believed him and ate the tree's fruit. She gave some to Adam and he ate it. Suddenly, they knew they were wrong. For the first time they were afraid to meet God.

Find It in the Bible
GENESIS 2:20–3:7

DAY 5
ADAM AND EVE LEAVE THE GARDEN

God walked in the cool garden breeze. But Adam and Eve were hiding among the trees. "Where are you?" called God.

"I heard you and was afraid," the man answered. "So I hid from you."

"Did you eat from the tree I warned you about?" asked God.

"The woman gave me the fruit. I ate it," the man said. So God spoke to the woman. "What have you done?"

"The serpent tricked me," she said, "and I ate." God turned to the serpent. "You have done this, so you will always crawl on your belly. You will hate the woman. She will also hate you. You and her child will fight. He will crush your head. You will bite him on the heel."

Then God told the woman, "You will have children. But you will be in pain when you do."

"Adam," God said, "you listened to her and ate from the tree. So you must work for all you get from the earth. You will sweat and suffer all your life. I made you out of dust. So you will turn back into dust."

Then God sent them out of the garden.

Find It in the Bible
GENESIS 3:8–24

DAY 6
CAIN MURDERS HIS BROTHER

Adam and Eve lived outside the garden until they died. A flaming sword guards the path to the Tree of Life. No one has gone back there since they left.

Eve gave birth to a baby boy named Cain. Her second baby was a boy named Abel.

When the boys became men they worked like their father. Cain was a farmer. Abel was a shepherd. One day Cain brought fruit to give to God. He worked to grow the fruit on his farm. Abel had a gift for God too. He gave a lamb that had been born in the field. God was happy with Abel's gift. But he refused Cain's gift.

Cain became angry, so God asked him, "Why are you angry? Be careful. Sin might catch you." Later, Cain killed Abel while he was walking in the field. God asked Cain, "Where is your brother?"

"I don't know," Cain answered. "Should I care for my brother?"

"What have you done?" God said. "Listen, Abel's blood is crying to me from the ground. You murdered Abel. You will always live under a curse."

So Cain went away from God. He lived east of Eden in the land of Nod.

Find It in the Bible
Genesis 3:23–4:16

DAY 7
NOAH BUILDS THE ARK

A long time passed after Cain killed Abel. The land was full of people. God looked at the world he had made. The people were wicked. God said, "I am sorry I made these people."

But God saw one good man named Noah. He told Noah, "I am going to wipe out the people I made. They will die with all things on earth. Only you are living right. So you and your family will be saved." Then God told Noah to build a huge boat called an ark. This ark was as big as a three-story building. "I am going to flood the earth with water," God said, "All the people and all the animals will drown."

"Noah," God went on, "bring two of every kind of animal into the ark. Gather food for them and for yourself. Then go into the ark with your family. In seven days I will send rain. The rain will fall for forty days. Everything I created will be wiped off the earth." And Noah did all the things God told him to do.

Find It in the Bible
GENESIS 6:1–7:5

DAY 8
NOAH LIVES IN THE ARK

Noah was six hundred years old when the rain started. Rain fell for forty days and forty nights. It rained like windows in the sky were opened. But the window in the ark was closed. Noah was safe inside and could not see out. One day, Noah sent out a dove. The dove came back with an olive leaf. So Noah knew the earth was drying out at last.

"Bring your family and all the animals out," God called. Gladly Noah came out. He had lived in the ark for over a year.

Find It in the Bible
GENESIS 7:6–8:19

DAY 9
THE RAINBOW OF GOD'S PROMISE

The flood was over. Every living thing on earth was killed. Only the animals and people in the ark came through alive. Noah knew what he should do first. He built an altar and gave gifts to God. This way Noah thanked God for saving his family.

God made a promise: "Never again will a flood destroy all life. The four seasons will come and go forever. The earth is yours, Noah. Rule it well."

Suddenly, the first rainbow curved through the sky. Now every time there is a rainbow, people remember God's promise to Noah.

Find It in the Bible
GENESIS 8:20–9:17

DAY 10
GOD APPEARS TO ABRAHAM

Once there was a city called Ur. God appeared to a man who lived there named Abraham. "Leave this place," God said. "Go to the land I will show you." And God made a promise to Abraham: "I will make your family a great people. I will bless you and make your name great. Everyone on earth will be blessed because of you."

Abraham left Ur with his family. Together, they traveled over hills and rivers to a land called Canaan. They camped by a big oak tree at Moreh. There God appeared to Abraham again. "I will give this land to all your children," he said. Abraham built an altar and worshiped God.

Traveling with Abraham was his nephew Lot. They went many places together in Canaan. At Bethel, Lot's shepherds and Abraham's shepherds were fighting. So Abraham invited Lot to choose another place to live. Near the Jordan River was a place called Sodom. Lot chose to live there. He thought it looked like the garden of God. But the people in Sodom were wicked and hated God.

Abraham lived in Canaan, the land God had promised to him.

Find It in the Bible
GENESIS 12:1–13:18

DAY 11
GOD MAKES A PROMISE

God came to Abraham again one night by the oak trees at Hebron. "Don't be afraid Abraham," he said. "I will keep you safe and give you a great reward."

"But, Lord," said Abraham, "I am old and don't have a son. Who will get this reward?" God took Abraham outside. "Look up. Try to count the stars," he said. "I promise that you will have more children than there are stars. This land called Canaan will be theirs."

Abraham believed God. And God said Abraham was right because he believed.

Find It in the Bible
GENESIS 15:1–18

DAY 12
SARAH LAUGHS AT GOD

It was a hot day by the oaks of Mamre. Abraham was sitting in the shade near his tent. Looking up, he saw God and two angels standing nearby. They looked just like men. Abraham and his wife, Sarah, rushed to make lunch for them.

"Where is your wife?" God asked. "She is going to have a child soon." In the tent, Sarah heard this and laughed. She was much too old to have children. "Why does she laugh?" God asked. "Nothing is too difficult for me. At the right time, she will have a baby."

Find It in the Bible
Genesis 18:1–15

DAY 13
FIRE RAINS ON SODOM

While God talked with Abraham, the angels left Mamre. That night they found Lot sitting by Sodom's gate. They had come to destroy that sinful place. First the angels warned Lot to leave. But Lot was in no hurry to get away. So the angels grabbed his hand. They rushed him out with his wife and daughters. They warned, "Run for your life into the hills. Don't look back."

God rained fire on Sodom. Smoke covered the valley. But Lot's wife looked back at the city. She turned into a pillar of salt. Her family kept running.

Find It in the Bible
GENESIS 19:1–26

ABRAHAM'S TWO SONS

After Sodom was destroyed, Abraham moved his camp nearer to the sea. There, when Abraham was one hundred years old, God kept his promise. Sarah gave birth to a baby boy. They were very happy and had a big feast. They named their son Isaac. His name means "laughing" because Sarah had laughed at God. And Sarah said, "God has brought laughter for me. Everyone who hears will laugh with me."

There were now two boys in Abraham's tent. One was Sarah's new baby, Isaac. The other was Ishmael. He was the son of Sarah's maid, Hagar. Ishmael did not like Isaac or treat him well. This made Sarah angry. She told Abraham, "Send away Hagar and her son. I don't want Ishmael to have what belongs to Isaac."

Abraham was very sad about this. Ishmael was his son, too. But God said, "Abraham, don't worry about Hagar and her son. Do what Sarah says. It's better that Isaac lives alone with you. Everything that is yours will belong to him someday. I'll take care of Ishmael. He'll be the father of a great family just like Isaac."

The next morning Abraham sent Hagar and Ishmael away.

Find It in the Bible
GENESIS 21:1–14

DAY 15
ISHMAEL'S DESERT JOURNEY

Early in the morning, Hagar and Ishmael left Abraham's tent. He gave them bread and a bottle of water for their trip. But the water ran out. Hagar didn't want Ishmael to die in the desert sun. There Hagar broke down and cried. But the angel of God called to Hagar from heaven. "Don't be afraid, Hagar. Lift up your son and hold him. He'll have a great family." Then God showed her a well of water, and they drank.

Ishmael grew up, and God was with him. He lived to become a hunter in the desert.

Find It in the Bible
GENESIS 21:14–20

ABRAHAM OFFERS ISAAC TO GOD

Meanwhile, God spoke to Abraham: "Take Isaac and go to Mount Moriah." Abraham loved Isaac. "There," God went on, "slay Isaac as a gift to me."

Abraham obeyed. They traveled three days to the mountain. Abraham put Isaac on an altar. Isaac asked, "Where is the lamb for God's gift?"

"God will give us a lamb," Abraham answered. He raised the knife to slay his son. Then God's angel stopped him: "I know you fear God. You'd slay your only son for him." Abraham saw a ram for God's gift stuck in a bush. So Isaac lived.

Find It in the Bible
GENESIS 22:1–19

THE SEARCH FOR ISAAC'S WIFE

Isaac grew up and was old enough to be married. It was Abraham's job to find a wife for Isaac. So Abraham sent his servant, Eliezer, back to his homeland. He wanted Isaac to marry a woman from his own family. Abraham knew this was best because they also worshiped God.

Eliezer took ten camels and many gifts. He traveled to the city of Nahor and stopped at the city well. There Eliezer prayed he would find the right woman for Isaac. He looked up and saw a beautiful young woman. Eliezer bowed to her and said, "Will you give me a drink?"

"Yes," the woman said. "I will water your camels, too." Eliezer wondered, "Is this the woman for Isaac?"

"What is your name?" he asked.

"I am Rebekah. My father is Bethuel." Bethuel was Abraham's brother. "Come," she said. "Stay at our house."

Eliezer thanked God. His prayer was answered. Rebekah was Isaac's cousin and part of Abraham's family. Eliezer gave Rebekah gold earrings and bracelets as gifts. He told her he was from Abraham's house. Rebekah invited Eliezer home to meet her father and family.

Find It in the Bible
GENESIS 24:1–27

REBEKAH MARRIES ISAAC

Rebekah ran home and told her parents about Eliezer. She showed them his gifts. Her brother Laban asked Eliezer to eat with them. But Eliezer said, "First I must tell you why I came here.

"My master is Abraham," Eliezer said. "God has blessed him. He is very rich. Abraham sent me here. I promised to find a wife for his son, Isaac. I prayed that God would show me the right woman." Then he told them what happened at the well.

Rebekah's father and brother agreed that she should marry Isaac. "God wants this to happen," they said.

Then Eliezer gave rich gifts to Rebekah and her family. That night they enjoyed a great feast. The next morning came. Rebekah's father asked her, "Will you go with this man?" She answered, "I will go." Rebekah's family blessed her and she left with Eliezer.

One evening Isaac was walking in the field. He saw Eliezer's camels coming with his bride. Rebekah also saw Isaac. Isaac loved Rebekah, and they were married in Sarah's tent.

Find It in the Bible
GENESIS 24:28–67

ESAU SELLS HIS BIRTHRIGHT

Like his father Abraham, Isaac lived in the land of Canaan. His wife Rebekah could not have children. So Isaac prayed and God answered his prayer. Rebekah gave birth to twin boys. She named them Esau and Jacob.

Esau was born first. He would get twice as much as Jacob when Isaac died. This was called the birthright.

Jacob grew to be a quiet man, living in the tents. Esau became a hunter in the fields. When Esau brought meat from the hunt, he gave some to Isaac. So Isaac loved Esau more than Jacob. But Rebekah liked the wise and careful Jacob.

One day Esau came in from the fields hungry and tired. Since it was time for dinner, Jacob cooked a pot of soup. "Please give me some soup," Esau asked.

"Will you trade your birthright for some soup?" Jacob asked.

"Why not?" answered Esau. "I am about to die of hunger. If I do die, I won't need my birthright." And Esau promised Jacob his birthright.

Jacob was selfish with Esau. This was not right. But Esau was foolish to sell his birthright. This was wrong.

Find It in the Bible
GENESIS 25:21–34

DAY 20
JACOB STEALS ESAU'S BLESSING

In time, Isaac became very old. One day he said to Esau, "I want to give you my blessing before I die. Hunt an animal and cook the meat for me. You know I love this. Then I will bless you." But Esau knew he had sold Jacob this blessing for some soup.

Nearby, Rebekah was listening. Quickly she cooked some meat. She gave it to Jacob. "Take this to your father. He is blind. So pretend you are Esau. Then you will get the blessing." Jacob did this. Though it was wrong, he stole Esau's blessing.

Find It in the Bible
GENESIS 27:1–38

DAY 21
JACOB'S DREAM AT BETHEL

After Esau lost his blessing he wanted to kill Jacob. Rebekah heard of this and said, "Jacob, hurry to your uncle Laban's."

Jacob rushed away alone. All he carried was a walking stick. At Bethel, he lay down to sleep. A stone was Jacob's pillow. In a dream he saw a ladder with angels on it. God blessed him saying, "I'm your father's God. This land is yours and your children's. The world will be blessed because of your family."

When he woke up, Jacob said, "This place is God's house. It's the gate of heaven."

Find It in the Bible
GENESIS 27:41–28:22

DAY 22
JACOB'S MARRIAGE

Jacob traveled to the city of Haran. There he found the same well where Eliezer met his mother, Rebekah. A young woman herded her sheep to the well for water. This was Rachel, the daughter of Jacob's uncle Laban. Jacob was so happy to meet her that he wept. And he fell in love with Rachel there.

Laban welcomed Jacob into his house. Soon Jacob told Laban, "I'll work seven years to marry Rachel."

Laban replied, "Better that Rachel marry you than a stranger."

Seven years passed. It seemed like only days to Jacob because he loved Rachel so. The day of the wedding came. The bride wore a thick veil. But when Jacob lifted the veil, it wasn't Rachel. Jacob had married Leah, Rachel's older sister. Jacob didn't love her. He'd been cheated because Laban wanted the older sister married first.

Then Jacob worked seven more years for Laban. Finally, he married Rachel. In those times men often had two wives.

Jacob lived with Laban twenty-one years. He had eleven sons there. Only one named Joseph was Rachel's son. Jacob loved him best.

Find It in the Bible
GENESIS 29:1–30:24

JACOB TRAVELS HOME

While he was with Laban, Jacob became rich. He had been wise and careful in his work. At last, he decided to go back to Canaan. While Laban was away, Jacob packed up his big family. He gathered his great herd of animals and began the journey.

When Laban found out, he was sad. Laban wanted Jacob to stay and work for him. So Laban and his men set out after Jacob. But in a dream, God told Laban, "Don't harm Jacob."

Laban caught up with Jacob in the hills of Gilead. There they made a promise to each other. They ate together by a pile of stones named "Witness." They promised not to harm each other. Both men knew that God was watching. So Jacob set up a big rock and called it "Watchtower."

In the morning, Laban kissed his daughters, blessed his grandchildren, and returned home.

Frightening news came. Esau was coming to meet Jacob with four hundred men. Would Esau kill him? In fear, Jacob divided everyone into two groups for safety. Shepherds went ahead with many animals as gifts for Esau. Jacob stayed behind alone to pray.

Find It in the Bible
GENESIS 31:17–32:22

GOD WRESTLES WITH JACOB

While he was alone, a man grabbed Jacob, and they wrestled until dawn. When he could not win, the man broke Jacob's hip.

"Let me go," the man said.

"I won't let you go unless you bless me," replied Jacob.

"What is your name?"

"Jacob."

"Not anymore," the man said. "It's now Israel."

"Why?" asked Jacob.

"You've wrestled with God and have won."

Then Jacob asked him, "What is your name?" The man only answered, "Why do you want to know?" Then he blessed Jacob.

Jacob said, "I've seen God's face and have lived."

Find It in the Bible
GENESIS 32:24–32

JOSEPH THE DREAMER

Jacob made peace with Esau and returned to Canaan. Soon another child was born to Rachel named Benjamin. But Jacob mourned because his lovely Rachel died.

Of all his sons, Jacob loved Joseph best. He rewarded Joseph with a beautiful coat of many colors. Joseph's brothers were jealous. They wished they could have such a coat.

One day Joseph said to his brothers, "Listen to the dreams I've had." When Joseph told them the dreams, his brothers knew their meaning: They would someday bow down to Joseph. The brothers hated Joseph because of his dreams.

Find It in the Bible
GENESIS 37:1–11

DAY 26
THE DREAMER IS SOLD AS A SLAVE

The sons of Jacob were tending flocks in the fields. Jacob wondered, "Are my sons safe?" He sent Joseph to find out. The brothers saw Joseph's brightly colored coat far off. "Look, here comes the dreamer," one announced.

"Let's kill him," another said, "and throw his body in a pit. We'll say a wild animal ate him."

"Good idea," said a third. "Then we'll see what happens to his dreams."

But Reuben, the oldest son, said, "No. Let's not kill him. Just throw him in the pit to die." Reuben planned to rescue Joseph later. So the brothers stole Joseph's pretty coat and dumped him in a pit.

Reuben left and was absent when a caravan of Ishmaelites came. The brothers sold Joseph to them for twenty silver pieces. The caravan carried Joseph to Egypt.

When Reuben returned, he cried, "The boy is gone; what shall I do?" The brothers decided to lie to Jacob. They stained Joseph's coat with animal blood. Jacob thought Joseph was killed.

"I will weep for my son the rest of my life," Jacob cried.

Find It in the Bible
GENESIS 37:12–35

DAY 27
JOSEPH THE SLAVE

The caravan carried Joseph south to Egypt, and a man named Potiphar bought Joseph. This man was a leader in Egypt's army.

God was with Joseph, though he was a slave. Potiphar saw his good work and liked him. He put Joseph in charge of his whole house. Potiphar's wife was also friendly to Joseph. But once he wouldn't do a wicked thing for her. So she lied to her husband about Joseph. Potiphar locked Joseph in prison like a criminal.

But God was with Joseph in prison. The jailer soon began to like Joseph. He even put Joseph in charge of the whole prison.

The king's butler and baker were there in prison. Both had dreams while they were sleeping. "What do our dreams mean?" they wondered.

"Maybe my God will tell me what they mean," Joseph said. And God did: The butler would be freed from prison. "When you are free," Joseph said, "Tell the king I'm here. Ask him to set me free."

The meaning of the baker's dream was sad: "You will be hanged for your crime," said Joseph.

And the men's dreams came true.

Find It in the Bible
GENESIS 39:1–40:22

DAY 28
PHARAOH SENDS FOR JOSEPH

Two years passed. The butler forgot about Joseph. Then Pharaoh, Egypt's king, dreamed dreams. "I must know what they mean," he thought.

Pharaoh called his magicians. All they said was, "We don't know what your dreams mean." Then the butler remembered Joseph.

"A young man is locked in your dungeon," he said. "He told me the meaning of my dream." Quickly Pharaoh sent for Joseph. First Joseph washed, then he went to Pharaoh.

"I've heard that you tell the meaning of dreams," said Pharaoh.

"I don't do this," Joseph replied. "God will give you the answer."

Find It in the Bible
GENESIS 40:23–41:16

THE MEANING OF PHARAOH'S DREAMS

What is the dream you have dreamed?" Joseph asked Pharaoh.

"I saw seven fat cows eating grass by the river," said Pharaoh. "Then seven skinny cows came. They ate the fat cows. But they were just as skinny as before they ate. Then I woke up.

"I fell asleep and dreamed again," Pharaoh went on. "I saw seven full heads of grain. They were all on one stalk. Another stalk grew next to that one. It had seven poor heads of grain. These thin heads swallowed the good heads of grain. But after this they were just as poor as before."

"The two dreams mean the same thing," Joseph told him. "God is showing you what he will do in Egypt. Seven years of very good crops will come soon. Then there will be seven years with no food. The time of good crops will be forgotten.

"Pharaoh should find a wise and able man to help Egypt," Joseph continued. "This man must save part of the crops from the good years. Then your people will have food when there are no crops. If someone can do this, the people of Egypt will not die."

Find It in the Bible
GENESIS 41:17–36

DAY 30
PHARAOH HONORS JOSEPH

Pharaoh asked his servants, "Can we find anyone like this young man? The spirit of God is in him." Then he looked at Joseph. "God has shown you all this. There is no one wiser than you. You shall be in charge of my palace and my country. I'm greater only because I'm king."

Then Pharaoh gave his own ring to Joseph. The best clothes were brought for him. A gold chain was placed on his neck. Joseph rode in his own chariot. Wherever he went the people bowed to him.

Find It in the Bible
GENESIS 41:37–45

DAY 31
JACOB'S SONS VISIT JOSEPH
PART ONE

Joseph was thirty years old when he began to serve Pharaoh. In the years when the crops were good, Joseph saved food. There was so much food saved, it couldn't be counted. During those years Joseph married and had two sons, Manasseh and Ephraim.

Then the good years in Egypt ended. The seven years with no food began and the Egyptians were hungry. They went to Pharaoh for food. He said, "Go to Joseph and do what he says." Joseph opened all the storehouses and sold food to the Egyptians. In fact, the whole world came to Joseph for food.

In Canaan, Jacob heard of the food in Egypt. He told his sons, "Go down and buy food for us. Then we won't starve." So all the brothers but Benjamin went down to Egypt.

Joseph sold food to everyone who came to Egypt to buy. Jacob's sons went to see Joseph like everyone else. They came into the room and bowed down before him. When he saw them, Joseph knew they were his brothers. Twenty-three years before they had sold him into slavery. The brothers did not know who Joseph was.

Find It in the Bible
GENESIS 41:46–42:7

JACOB'S SONS VISIT JOSEPH
PART TWO

Now, as in Joseph's boyhood dreams, his brothers bowed before him. "Who are you?" Joseph asked. "Where do you come from?"

"We've come from Canaan to buy food," they answered.

"No, you didn't," Joseph said. "You're spies. You want to see how weak Egypt has become."

"No, sir. We are twelve brothers," they said. The youngest is at home. One has died."

"You must prove you aren't spies," Joseph answered. "Someone must go back and bring your youngest brother here." Then the rest were locked up.

Three days later, Joseph spoke: "One of you must remain. The others may leave with your family's food. But bring your youngest brother back to me. Then I'll know you're not spies." The youngest brother, Benjamin, was Rachel's son, like Joseph.

Joseph chose Simeon to stay in Egypt. Reuben told the others, "This has happened because of what you did to Joseph." They didn't know Joseph overheard them. He went away and wept. He knew his brothers were sorry for what they had done.

Find It in the Bible
GENESIS 42:6–24

JACOB'S FOOD RUNS OUT

Reuben and his brothers bought bags filled with food. But Joseph wanted his brothers to have the food for free. Their money was put back in their food bags. Sadly, they left Simeon in Egypt and went home.

On the way home, they found the money. "Look what God has done to us!" they cried. But they couldn't go back to Egypt.

At home, they told Jacob what had happened. "First Joseph died and now Simeon is gone," he cried. "And you want to take Benjamin from me. You've made my hair gray. If I lose Benjamin, I'll die."

With Jacob's large family, the food was soon gone, and the brothers needed to get some more.

"We can't go unless Benjamin comes along," they said.

"If he must go, then he must," replied Jacob. "But take special gifts and twice as much money. It was a mistake that the money was in your bags. May God Almighty have mercy on you in Egypt."

So Jacob's sons took Benjamin and returned to Egypt. Soon they were bowing down to Joseph again.

Find It in the Bible
GENESIS 42:25–43:15

JACOB'S SONS VISIT JOSEPH
PART THREE

Joseph saw his little brother, Benjamin, with the others. "Bring them to my house for a feast," he told the servants.

Jacob's sons were afraid to go to Joseph's house. "We brought the money back that was in our bags," they said.

"God gave you that money," a servant told them. Then he brought Simeon out to them. When Joseph came in, the brothers bowed to the ground.

Joseph asked, "Is your father well? Is he alive?" They answered, "Our father is well." Joseph looked with love at Benjamin. This was his little brother, his mother's son. He had to go out and weep. He was so happy.

So they had a big feast together. But the brothers still did not know Joseph's secret.

Then Joseph gave them much food and put money in their bags again. He hid his special silver cup in Benjamin's bag. Joseph did this to make them return.

So Jacob's sons returned to Egypt. Joseph said, "The one who stole my cup will be my slave." This was Benjamin, the brother Joseph loved.

Find It in the Bible
GENESIS 43:16–44:17

DAY 35
A JOYOUS FAMILY REUNION

Judah was one of Jacob's sons. He was afraid, but he spoke to Joseph: "Benjamin's father is old. He'll die if his son doesn't return. His brother has already been killed by beasts. Let me stay. Then the boy can go back to his father."

Then Joseph could not keep his secret any longer. He cried out, "I'm Joseph, your brother! You sold me into Egypt. But God wanted this. I've given food to all the world." And he wept on Benjamin's shoulder. Then they all kissed and hugged and talked. All of Pharaoh's palace was glad.

Find It in the Bible
GENESIS 44:18–45:16

ISRAEL MOVES TO EGYPT

Pharaoh was happy that Joseph had found his family. He said, "Your brothers can move their families to the best land in Egypt." Joseph sent his brothers back to Canaan with money and new clothes. He sent his father donkeys loaded with grain and bread.

When they came to Canaan, the brothers ran to Jacob. "Joseph lives!" they shouted. "He rules in Egypt." Jacob wouldn't believe them. When they explained, he said, "Enough. I must see Joseph before I die."

Long before this God had named Jacob "Israel." And Israel gathered his family and set out for Egypt. On the way he gave gifts to God. God spoke to Israel: "Don't be afraid to go to Egypt. I'll go down with you. Your family will become a great nation there. I'll bring them up to Canaan again." Seventy people in Israel's family moved to Egypt.

Israel came to Joseph. "I've seen that you're alive," he said. "Now I can die in peace."

Pharaoh soon met Israel. "How old are you?" he asked.

"My life has been short and hard," said Israel. "I am 130 years old." And he blessed Pharaoh.

Find It in the Bible
GENESIS 45:25–47:10

THE DEATHS OF ISRAEL AND JOSEPH

Israel and his children lived in Goshen, which had rich farmland. Israel lived almost 150 years. As he was dying, he blessed his twelve sons, saying, "Don't bury me in Egypt. Bury me in Canaan with my father, Isaac, and grandfather, Abraham."

And so there was a great funeral for Jacob. Israel's children carried his body to Canaan. There he was buried in the cave at Machpelah near Mamre.

When Jacob's sons came back to Egypt, they were afraid. "Is Joseph still mad that we sold him?" they worried. They sent him a message: "Please forgive us for our crime."

"What you did was bad," Joseph told them. "But God used it for good. Look at all the children of Israel. Don't worry. I'll always provide for you and your families."

Joseph lived 110 years. Before he died, he said to his brothers, "God will come and take you back to Canaan. Instead, when you go, carry my bones back with you." So they kept Joseph's stone coffin. They knew that someday they would carry it back to their own land.

Find It in the Bible
GENESIS 47:27–50:26

DAY 38
EGYPT PUNISHES ISRAEL

The people of Israel increased and filled Goshen. Then a new king ruled. He didn't remember Joseph. This pharaoh was afraid that Israel would become more powerful than Egypt. He made Israel's people into slaves. Israel was forced to make bricks for Pharaoh's cities. They had to give Egypt most of their food. In spite of this cruel treatment, Israel grew larger.

Pharaoh then made a terrible law. All the baby boys born in Israel must be killed. But their nurses let them live. So Pharaoh ordered the babies to be thrown into the river.

Find It in the Bible
Exodus 1:6–22

DAY 39
MOSES IS SAVED FROM DEATH

A baby boy was born in Goshen. His mother saw that he was a fine boy. She hid him from the Egyptians for three months. When she couldn't hide him any longer, she wove a basket. It was made so no water could leak into it. She put the boy in the basket. Then she floated it among the reeds by the river.

Pharaoh's daughter bathed in the river at that place. She discovered the basket and felt sorry for the crying baby. She kept him and named him Moses.

Find It in the Bible
EXODUS 2:1–10

DAY 40
A PRINCE BECOMES A SHEPHERD

Moses grew up in Pharaoh's palace. There he learned all the wisdom of Egypt. He did powerful deeds. But he loved his own people, Israel. They were still slaves.

Moses wanted to help Israel. But he could do nothing. Besides, Israel did not want his help. Pharaoh was angry with Moses for trying to help. So Moses ran far away from Egypt to Midian in Arabia.

He was resting there by a well. Young women were trying to water their flocks. When rough men stopped them, Moses helped the women. These were the daughters of Jethro, priest of Midian. Moses was invited to stay in Jethro's house. He married Jethro's daughter, Zipporah, and herded Jethro's flocks.

For forty years, Moses had lived in Egypt. There he was a wise and powerful prince. Now he shepherded another man's sheep. He lived on the far side of the desert. "I'm a stranger living in a strange land," Moses said.

Meanwhile, Israel cried and groaned in slavery. God heard them. He remembered his promises to Abraham, Isaac, and Jacob. God saw Israel in Egypt and understood their troubles.

Find It in the Bible
EXODUS 2:11–25

GOD APPEARS IN A BURNING BUSH

Moses had his flock on Mount Horeb. There, God appeared to him as a flame of fire in a bush. Moses saw the bush burning but not burned up. Moses wondered why the bush didn't burn up.

God called from the bush, "Moses, Moses."

"I'm here," Moses answered.

"Come no closer," God warned. "Take off your sandals. You're standing on holy ground. I am your ancestor's God—the God of Abraham, of Isaac, and of Jacob."

Moses hid his face and couldn't look at God.

Find It in the Bible
EXODUS 3:1–6

MOSES IS SENT TO EGYPT

I've seen Israel's suffering in Egypt." God spoke from the burning bush. "I've come to set them free from Egypt. I'll bring them up to Canaan. It's a place that's flowing with milk and honey. Come on, Moses, I'm sending you to Pharoah. Bring my people out of Egypt."

Moses said, "I'm nobody. How can I go to Pharoah and rescue Israel?"

"I'll be with you," God answered. "Bring them out; worship me on this mountain."

"But," Moses said, "they'll ask, 'What is God's name?' What do I tell them?"

"Say, 'I AM sent me to you.' Tell Israel, 'The God of your ancestors has sent me to you—the God of Abraham, of Isaac, and of Jacob.' "

"What if they still don't believe me?" Moses asked.

God told him, "Throw down your shepherd's staff." Moses did, and his staff became a snake. "Do this," God said, "and other signs I'll show you. I'm sending your brother Aaron to help you."

So Moses and Aaron went to Goshen and talked with Israel's leaders. They believed. God had heard their cries. Together they bowed down and worshiped.

Find It in the Bible
Exodus 3:7–4:31

DAY 43
MOSES SPEAKS TO PHARAOH

Right away, Moses and Aaron went to Pharaoh. They said, "God is speaking to you through us. Let my people go so they can serve me." But Pharaoh got angry and made Israel suffer more.

Moses prayed to God, "Why did you send me to Pharaoh?" God told him, "Go back to Pharaoh. Show him the signs I gave you." So Moses and Aaron returned. Aaron threw down his staff. It became a snake. Pharaoh's magicians then did the same thing. But Aaron's staff swallowed up the magician's snakes.

Find It in the Bible
EXODUS 5:1–7:13

BLOOD AND FROGS IN EGYPT

God told Moses, "Pharaoh has a hard heart. He still won't let the people go. Take the staff that turned into a snake. Go to the Nile River. Tell Pharaoh that the Hebrews' God says, 'Let my people go.' Then hit the water with the staff. It will turn to blood. Do this so Pharaoh will know that I am God."

Moses and Aaron did this and the Nile River turned to blood. It smelled terrible and all the fish died. There was blood everywhere and no water to drink. But Pharaoh's heart was still hard.

Seven days later, God sent Moses and Aaron back to Pharaoh. "God says, 'Let my people go,' " they told him. But he wouldn't do it. So Aaron held his staff over the river. Frogs came up and covered Egypt. They even got into people's beds and ovens.

Pharaoh called to Moses, "Ask God to take away the frogs. Then I'll let Israel go." Moses did this and all the frogs died in one day. They were piled up in heaps and smelled terrible. But Pharaoh hardened his heart again. He didn't let the people go.

Find It in the Bible
EXODUS 7:14–8:15

DAY 45
THE TERRIBLE DAYS OF EGYPT

Pharaoh wouldn't let God's people go. So Aaron hit the ground with his staff. All the dust turned into fleas. They bit everyone. But it made no difference to Pharaoh.

Soon swarms of flies filled Egypt. Pharaoh softened. "You may go a short way. Worship God and come right back," he said. So God took the flies away. But then Pharaoh wouldn't let the people go.

So a terrible disease made all of Egypt's horses, cattle, and sheep die. Painful sores broke out on the Egyptians. But Pharaoh wouldn't obey. Hail fell on Egypt and killed everything outdoors. Grasshoppers came and ate everything that was left.

Finally, Egypt became dark for three days. People couldn't see each other or even move. And Pharaoh said, "Go out and worship. But your animals must stay behind."

"No," said Moses. "We must bring our animals to sacrifice."

"Then you can't go," replied Pharaoh. "I will kill you if I see you again."

"This is true," answered Moses. "I'll never see you again."

Find It in the Bible
EXODUS 8:16–10:29

DAY 46
GOD'S PASSOVER

None of the terrible things that had happened to Egypt hurt Israel.

God said to Moses, "In a few days you are all to leave Egypt. Be ready to go when the time comes. This month is the beginning of the new year for Israel," God went on. "I want every family to find a perfect lamb. On the fourteenth day of the month, they must kill it. Take its blood and put it on the door frame. There must be blood on every door. Then roast the lamb and have a feast. Eat it fast, and be ready to travel. It is my passover.

"I will pass through Egypt that night. The oldest boy in every family will be killed. The blood on your doors will be a sign. When I see the blood, I'll pass over your house. Your boys will not die when I strike Egypt. Always remember this day and keep this feast."

Israel did what they were told. That night came, and a great cry went up all over Egypt. In every house the oldest son died. But Israel had the lambs' blood on their doors. The destroying angel passed over them.

Find It in the Bible
EXODUS 12:1–30

DAY 47
ISRAEL'S EXODUS

Pharaoh woke up that night and found his own son dead. All of Egypt was crying. In every house, someone had died. Pharaoh called Moses, "Take Israel and get away from my people. Take everything you have and be gone."

Israel had lived in Egypt 430 years. Six hundred thousand men began the exodus that night. Of course they had their wives and children with them. Their flocks and herds followed. They didn't forget to bring Joseph's coffin. When they came to Canaan, they buried Joseph as promised.

God was their leader. Israel could see the Lord ahead of them. In the daytime, there was a great cloud like a pillar. At night, they saw a pillar of fire. So they said, "The God of heaven and earth goes before us."

This great nation traveled southeast to the sea. They followed God in the pillar of cloud and of fire. But Pharaoh was sorry he'd let them go. Who would be his slaves? He led his army after them.

Israel faced the Red Sea. Mountains were on each side. Pharaoh and his army were close behind. Then Moses said, "Stand still and see how God will save you."

Find It in the Bible
EXODUS 12:30–14:14

ESCAPE THROUGH THE SEA

Trapped between the army and the Red Sea, Israel cried out. Moses said, "The Lord will fight for you" and lifted his staff over the sea. "You'll never see the Egyptians again."

All night an east wind blew. The water split in two and the sea became dry. Israel went into the sea on dry ground following the Lord. The water formed two walls.

The Egyptians chased after them. But the wheels fell from their chariots, and they tried to run. Just then, Moses lifted his staff again. The sea returned and the Egyptians drowned.

Find It in the Bible
EXODUS 14:15–30

DAY 49
THE SONG OF VICTORY

O n the other side of the Red Sea, Moses wrote a song. It is about God's victory over Egypt. Together, Israel sang the song. It begins like this:

I will sing to the Lord for his glorious victory.
He threw the horse and rider into the sea.
The Lord is my strength and my song.
He has become my salvation.

Now they were in a huge desert. As they traveled, they became thirsty. They found a pool, but the water was bad. They were angry and called it Marah which means "bitter." God told Moses, "Cut a tree and throw it in the water." This made the water fresh.

Find It in the Bible
EXODUS 15:1–25

DAY 50
FOOD RAINS FROM HEAVEN

After Marah, Israel came to a place of twelve fresh springs. There they rested under seventy palm trees. But soon they were in a hot dry desert with no food. Everybody whined at Moses. "We should have died in Egypt," they moaned. "That would be better than dying in this desert."

God spoke to Moses, too. "I'm going to rain food from heaven for you," he said. "Every day you'll go out and gather enough for that day." The next morning, they saw little white flakes like frost on the ground. "What is it?" they asked.

"This is the bread God has given you," Moses answered. "Gather as much of it as you need. Don't keep any leftovers. They'll spoil." Morning by morning they gathered as much as they needed. But when the sun got hot it melted on the ground. Some tried to keep it overnight. In the morning it was stinky and filled with worms.

Israel called this food "manna," which means "what is it?" Every day for the next forty years, they ate manna. They were never hungry. Manna stopped falling when Israel came to Canaan.

Find It in the Bible
Exodus 15:27–16:35

WATER SPRINGS FROM A ROCK

The people of Israel were traveling through a huge desert. Water was very hard to find. Their children cried for water. The people yelled at Moses, "Give us water! Did you bring us out of Egypt so we would die?"

So Moses called on God. "What shall I do? They may kill me over water."

"Bring the staff you used at the Red Sea," God said. "I'll be standing on the rock at Horeb. Hit the rock with your staff and water will flow out."

Moses did this and all Israel drank the water.

Find It in the Bible
EXODUS 17:1–7

MOSES, GOD, AND THE MOUNTAIN

The nation of Israel traveled for three months. They finally arrived at Mount Sinai. This great mountain rises straight up from the desert. It is near the place where Moses saw the burning bush. Here, in front of the mountain, Israel camped.

God spoke to Moses from the mountain. "Don't let the people touch this mountain. It is a holy place. Soon, they will all see me come to the mountain top."

Three days later all Israel came to the mountain to meet God. Sinai was wrapped in smoke. God had come down on it in fire. The whole mountain shook wildly and the people were terrified. A trumpet began to blast louder and louder. Moses spoke to God and God answered in thunder. The people thought they would die. "Don't let God speak to us anymore," they begged.

Moses entered the cloud and thick darkness on the mountain. God called him to the mountain top. He and God spoke together there for forty days. God told him about all the laws Israel should obey. God gave Moses two tablets made of stone. On these tablets God himself had written the Ten Commandments.

Find It in the Bible
EXODUS 19:1–24:18

DAY 53
WORSHIPING A GOLDEN CALF

The people of Israel wondered, "What's happened to Moses?" He had been on the mountain for weeks. Then they did a strange and wicked thing. They made themselves a god.

Aaron said, "Take off all your gold earrings. Bring them to me." He melted the gold and molded it in the shape of a calf.

"This is your god, O Israel," the people shouted. "It saved you out of Egypt." And Aaron built an altar to worship the calf. The next morning, a huge party began. The people ate and drank and danced all day.

Find It in the Bible
EXODUS 32:1–6

MOSES SMASHES THE GOLDEN CALF

H urry down the mountain," the Lord told Moses. "Your people have made an idol and are worshiping it. I'm about to destroy them all."

"O Lord, please change your mind," Moses prayed. "Remember Abraham, Isaac, and Jacob? You promised that their families would be like the stars in heaven. What about the land of Canaan that you promised to give them?" So the Lord changed his mind.

On the way down, Moses could hear the wild party below. He came near the camp. Then he could see the golden calf and the dancers. He became hot with anger. He threw the two stone tablets to the ground and they shattered.

Pushing through the crowd, Moses snatched the gold calf off the altar. He smashed it, burned it, and ground it to dust. "Who is on the Lord's side?" he demanded. The tribe of Levi stepped up. "Go through the camp. Kill the idol worshipers."

The men of Levi killed three thousand people that day. Moses prayed for God to forgive Israel. Then Moses went up the mountain with two new stone tablets.

Find It in the Bible
EXODUS 32:7–34:4

DAY 55
THE DAZZLING FACE OF MOSES

For the second time, Moses spent forty days with God. The Lord wrote his laws on the new tablets and talked with Moses.

Moses brought the tablets down the mountain. He didn't know that his face shone with God's light. His face was so dazzling that the people couldn't look at him.

Moses spoke to Israel about God's laws. He had to cover his face with a veil. The light hurt the eyes of the people when they saw him.

Find It in the Bible
EXODUS 34:5–35:1

THE TABERNACLE OF GOD

On the mountain, God told Moses his plan for Israel. He showed Moses the way to build a special kind of tent. In it the people would meet with God. This tent was called the tabernacle. They also called it the tent of meeting.

Moses called for an offering to the Lord. Everyone brought gold and cloth, fine leather, oil and spices, beautiful wood, and precious stones. All this was used in building the tabernacle. Many people were skilled carpenters and handy with their hands. They came to help build the tent of meeting.

This was an expensive, large, and beautiful tent. It was made of the best materials exactly like the Lord planned it. Its walls were boards covered with gold. Over these the tent was hung. It was blue, scarlet, and purple linen cloth. This was covered with skins and hides

Outside the tabernacle was a brass altar for offerings. There were beautiful pieces of special furniture inside. The entire tabernacle could be packed and carried on Israel's travels.

Finally, Moses and the people finished the tabernacle. The cloud that lead them out of Egypt covered the tent. God's glory filled the tabernacle.

Find It in the Bible
EXODUS 35:1–40:38

INSIDE THE TABERNACLE

Inside the tabernacle were two rooms: the holy place and the holy of holies. The entire tent was forty-five feet long, fifteen feet wide, and fifteen feet high.

In the holy place were three things: a gold table with twelve loaves of bread; a gold lampstand with seven lamps; and an altar for incense. The holy of holies was the inner room. Only the high priest could enter here. It held the ark of the covenant—a gold-covered box. Inside it were the two stone tablets. This room was God's dwelling place.

Find It in the Bible
EXODUS 35–40

GOD'S PRIESTS

God decided that Aaron and his sons would be priests. They would lead the worship and serve him. The high priest wore a beautiful robe and hat. On his chest was a covering of precious stones. The priests never wore shoes.

Only the priests could go inside the tent of meeting. There they filled the lamps with oil. These lamps were always burning. They kept fresh bread in the tent and burned incense. Aaron and his sons were members of the tribe of Levi. Other men in this tribe became the priests' helpers.

Find It in the Bible
EXODUS 27:20–28:5

THE SCAPEGOAT FOR SIN

Once a year came the day of atonement. Special animal sacrifices were given to God that day. These were meant to take away the people's sins.

There was an unusual ritual on the day of atonement. Two goats were chosen. These goats stood for the people of Israel and their sins. One goat was killed as a sacrifice to God for sin. The second goat was the scapegoat. He was set free in the wilderness. He could never find his way back to the camp. This meant that sins were taken away, never to return.

Find It in the Bible
LEVITICUS 16:7–10

DAY 60
SPIES IN THE LAND

Israel camped by Mount Sinai for almost a year. They built the tabernacle and Moses taught them God's law. At last God's cloud lifted from the tabernacle. This was the sign that they should continue their travels to Canaan.

They packed the tent of meeting and followed God. The pillar of cloud was their leader by day. The pillar of fire led them by night. At last they arrived and camped just outside Canaan at Kadesh.

Moses chose one man from each tribe, twelve in all. He sent them to spy in Canaan. "Go and see what the land is like. Find out if the tribes there are strong or weak. Be brave, and bring back some fruit from the land."

Forty days later the spies returned. They carried a huge bunch of grapes on two men's shoulders. "This land flows with milk and honey," they reported. "But the people are strong and the cities like forts. The men are so big that we felt like little grasshoppers."

The people were afraid of what they heard. They forgot all that God had done. He had promised to give them Canaan. But Israel refused to enter the land.

Find It in the Bible
NUMBERS 13:1–33

THE LONG DESERT JOURNEY

The people of Israel were complaining. "We should have died in Egypt or the desert. Why does God want us to die in a war in Canaan? Let's all go back to Egypt." Suddenly the glory of God flashed and shone from the tabernacle.

God spoke: "How long will this people disobey and despise me? They shall not enter Canaan. Instead they will all die in the desert. Their children will grow up, and only they will enter this good land. Tomorrow you must go back to the desert. You will wander there for forty years."

Then the people changed their minds. "No," they all said. "We'll not go back to the desert. We'll go straight into the land right now."

"You must not go into Canaan," Moses said. "God will not go with you." But they rushed to enter Canaan anyway. The tribes who lived there, the Canaanites and the Amorites, attacked them. Many Israelites were killed. So they finally turned back into the desert.

For forty years, they moved through the desert. The old men died and the young men were trained as warriors. Then they came back to Kadesh near Canaan where they began.

Find It in the Bible
NUMBERS 14:1–45

A SNAKE MADE OF BRASS

Once, in the desert, Israel complained against God and Moses. "Why did you bring us from Egypt to die?" they moaned. "We've no water, and we're sick of eating manna."

God became angry and he sent poisonous snakes into the camp. They bit many people who then died. Israel came to Moses and said, "We've sinned."

So God told Moses to make a snake out of brass. "Hang it on a pole," God said. "Whoever looks at it will not die."'

Moses did this. People bitten by a snake looked at the brass serpent and lived.

Find It in the Bible
NUMBERS 21:5–9

THE DEATH OF MOSES

Today I'm 120 years old," Moses told Israel. "The Lord has said that I'll not go into Canaan. So the time has come for me to die. But the Lord will go into the land with you. So be strong and brave, and always keep God's law. The Lord will not fail you nor leave you." Moses then went into the tabernacle to God. The pillar of cloud stood over the door of the tent.

That day Moses left the camp alone. He slowly climbed to the top of Mount Nebo. There he could see Canaan. God spoke to Moses. "This is the land I promised to Abraham, Isaac, and Jacob. You can look at it from here, but you can't go in." And Moses gazed at the promised land across the river.

Moses was still strong and his eyes were good. But he lay down on the mountain and died just as God wanted. No one was there to bury him, so God did the job. No one knows where he is buried. There was never again anyone like Moses. The Lord knew him face-to-face. And Israel mourned for thirty days.

Find It in the Bible
DEUTERONOMY 34:1–12

THE SUFFERING OF JOB

A man named Job lived east of Canaan. He was very rich, and also very good.

Once the angels were standing in front of God. Satan was there with them.

"Have you seen my servant Job?" God asked. "There's no one like him. He's blameless and right and rejects evil."

"Take away all he has. He'll curse you," Satan said.

"All right, Satan," God said. "Do what you want with him."

Soon trouble came to Job. His animals were driven away or killed with Job's shepherds. Then all his sons and daughters were killed. Their house fell in on them. All this happened in one day.

Job said, "I came into this world with nothing. I'll leave with nothing, too. The Lord gave me everything; he can take it away. The Lord's name is blessed."

God again said to Satan, "Have you seen Job? He's blameless and right."

"Give me power to make him sick. Then we'll see how good he is."

"All right, Satan," God said, "just don't kill him."

Find It in the Bible
JOB 1:1–2:6

DAY 65
THE PRAYER OF JOB

Satan made sores come onto Job's body. This was very painful. But Job wouldn't speak against God.

"You should curse God and die," his wife said.

"Should we take the good from the Lord and not the bad?" he answered.

Job's friends thought God had made the bad things happen. "Maybe Job has done evil," they said, "and this is punishment." Job didn't believe this. He knew God's goodness.

"You don't speak the truth about me," God told them. "But Job does."

So Job prayed for his friends. God returned to Job twice as much as he'd lost.

Find It in the Bible
Job 2:7–42:17

DAY 66
JOSHUA, JERICHO, AND
THE JORDAN RIVER

After Moses died, God chose Joshua. "You must take the place of Moses and lead Israel. Don't wait. Lead them across the Jordan River. I will give them the land I promised to their ancestors. Be strong and brave. I will be with you just like I was with Moses."

Then Joshua gave orders to Israel's leaders: "Tell everyone to get ready. In three days we are going to cross the Jordan. You will take the land God has given to you." Israel moved its camp to the east bank of the Jordan River.

At that time of year, the river was overflowing its banks. Only a strong man could swim across, and Israel had no boats. Across the river, the people could see the strong walls of Jericho. Before they could take the land, they had to take this city.

Joshua chose two brave and wise men to be spies. "Go find out all you can about Jericho and the land beyond." So these men swam the river and entered Jericho. They spent that night in the house of a woman named Rahab.

Find It in the Bible
JOSHUA 1:1–2:1

THE WOMAN WITH THE SCARLET ROPE

Jericho's king heard of the spies in Rahab's house. He sent soldiers to capture them. Rahab rushed to hide them. She then sent the soldiers to look for them elsewhere.

Before the spies slept, she said, "I know God has given you this land. Promise me that Israel won't kill my family."

"We promise you this because you've saved our lives."

Rahab let down a scarlet rope for them to escape. "Israel will see this red rope hanging out your window," they said. "It will be a sign for them not to harm you."

Find It in the Bible
Joshua 2:2–24

THE JORDAN IS CUT OFF

The spies reported to Joshua and Israel packed to travel. Joshua gave the order, and they moved toward the rushing river. Priests led the way carrying the ark of the covenant.

God told Joshua, "The feet of the priests will stand in the river. Then the water flowing down will be cut off." So the priests walked into the Jordan, and the river stood still. Up river, the water piled up in a heap. The entire nation of Israel crossed the Jordan on dry ground. When the priests walked out, the river began to flow again.

Find It in the Bible
JOSHUA 3:1–17

THE WALL OF JERICHO FALLS

God said to Joshua, "I've given you the city of Jericho." He then told Joshua how to defeat the city. It was done God's way.

Israel's army went to the city as if to fight. With them went priests holding trumpets made of ram's horns. The ark of the covenant was carried along as they marched. For six days, while the trumpets blew, they marched around the city once. On the seventh day, they circled the city seven times. When Joshua ordered, Israel shouted! Then Jericho's wall fell down flat, and they took the city.

Find It in the Bible
JOSHUA 6:1–27

GIBEON LIES TO ISRAEL

T he tribes in Canaan heard about Israel at Jericho. They prepared to fight the invaders. Not far from Israel's camp lived the Gibeonites. They knew they couldn't fight Israel, so they decided to make peace.

The men of Gibeon came to Joshua wearing worn and ragged clothes. "We have come from a far country. The things you did at Jericho are well known. We want to be your friends and make peace."

Joshua and the elders of Israel didn't ask God what to do. They agreed not to destroy the Gibeonites. Later, Joshua learned that their cities were very near. At first, the leaders of Israel were angry. They wanted to break the agreement with Gibeon.

Joshua called them back to Israel's camp. "Why did you lie to us?" he asked. The Gibeonites answered, "We heard God had promised Moses this land. We were afraid for our lives. But now we are in your hands. Do what you like with us."

That day Joshua made them woodcutters and water carriers for Israel. From that time the people of Gibeon served the camp of Israel.

Find It in the Bible
JOSHUA 9:1–27

THE WAR FOR CANAAN

The largest city near Israel's camp was Jerusalem. There the people worshiped idols which are false gods. The king of Jerusalem joined with four nearby cities to destroy Gibeon. "They made peace with our enemy, Israel," he said.

Soon the people of Gibeon heard this. They went to Joshua and said, "Come quickly and help us. Hurry before it is too late. The whole country is coming to kill us."

Joshua moved swiftly. He called out his army. All night they marched up the mountains. Suddenly, they came upon the five kings at Bethhoron. There they fought a great battle. The enemy panicked, and the Lord rained hailstones on their armies.

Israel destroyed the armies of the five kings. Then Joshua turned north to fight the kings there. At the lake of Merom, he defeated the northern kings.

There were six great marches and six battles in Israel's war for Canaan. Three were east of the Jordan River while Moses was alive. Joshua won the battles of Jericho, Bethhoron, and Merom west of the river. But many years passed before Israel won all the land.

Find It in the Bible
JOSHUA 10:1–11:23

THE LAND IS DIVIDED

God commanded Joshua to divide the land among the people. There were twelve tribes in Israel. One for each of the sons of Jacob. Two tribes and half of another had already been given their land. They lived on the other side of the Jordan River. This left nine and one-half tribes to be given land.

Judah was given the mountain country west of the Dead Sea. Simeon was on the south, toward the desert. Benjamin was north of Judah toward the Jordan River. In the middle of the country lived the tribe of Ephraim. This is where Joseph was finally buried. Ephraim was a son of Joseph. Joshua lived in Ephraim because he belonged to that tribe.

North of Ephraim lived the other half of the tribe of Manasseh. Four tribes lived in the northern part of the land. Issachar was in the south. Asher lived in the west by the sea. Zebulun was in the middle, in the mountains. Naphtali was in the north by what is now the Sea of Galilee.

The land was no longer called Canaan. It became known as the Land of Israel.

Find It in the Bible
JOSHUA 15:1–19:51

ISRAEL'S CITIES OF REFUGE

God told Moses to choose six cities for a special purpose. These were to be the cities of refuge.

People sometimes kill others by accident. If this happened in Israel they could be safe in these cities. This was a law of God that had been given by Moses. Before that, if someone killed another by accident, they too were killed. The dead man's relatives would kill them. It didn't matter that it was an accident.

For example, if an axe slipped and killed a man, the man holding the axe would have to pay with his life. Or there might be a hunting accident where a man was killed. The other hunter would be killed by the dead man's relatives. But Moses' new law brought justice to these cases.

When such an accident occurred, the innocent person could run to a refuge city. The elders there would decide if the death was an accident. Then the innocent man could live safely in the refuge city. When the high priest died, he could return to his first home. There he could live in peace without fear. This is one way Israel's laws made life better.

Find It in the Bible
JOSHUA 20:1–9

THE ALTAR BY THE RIVER

The tribe of Levi served as priests for Israel. They ministered at the tabernacle. They weren't given part of the land. Instead, they were given cities. The people of Levi served God part of the year. Then they went to their cities and worked.

Joshua had the tabernacle set up in Shiloh. This was near the center of the land. The people went to Shiloh three times a year to worship. It was the only place God allowed Israel to worship.

But the tribes on the east of the Jordan set up another altar. The other ten tribes were unhappy. Two places to worship meant that Israel was divided. God didn't want this. The tribes almost went to war with each other. But first the ten tribes asked, "Why do you have that new altar?"

The tribes east of the Jordan had a good answer. "Do you see that our altar is on your side of the river? We will show this to our children as a reminder. They'll remember that Israel is one people on two sides of a river. It isn't for worship. It's a reminder that the Lord is the God of us all."

Find It in the Bible
JOSHUA 22:1–34

THE LAST DAYS OF JOSHUA

Joshua was more than one hundred years old. So he called the leaders of the twelve tribes together. Joshua spoke to them in love. He told them their story beginning with Abraham. He reminded them of all the Lord had done. "Now," Joshua said, "fear the Lord. Serve him with all your heart."

The people said, "We'll do this."

So Joshua set up a huge stone by the oak in Shechem. "This stone stands for the fact that God has heard your promise."

Joshua died at age 110. Israel served God as long as the people remembered Joshua.

Find It in the Bible
JOSHUA 23:1–24:33

ISRAEL FORGETS GOD

L ater, everyone in Israel who knew Joshua died. The older people worshiped God, but the younger ones forgot him.

God told Israel to drive out the people living in Canaan. But Israel hadn't done this. The Canaanites didn't worship the Lord. They worshiped idols and false gods. God hates this.

Sadly, Israel forgot the God of their ancestors. They began to follow the gods of the people around them. They stopped worshiping at the tabernacle. Instead they worshiped a god named Baal.

God was very angry about this. He let Israel suffer for it. He left them so they were helpless. Israel's enemies attacked them and robbed them. Their grain, grapes, olive oil, and animals were gone.

At times, during their sufferings, Israel would remember God and cry out. God would find someone in Israel to be their judge. These judges were wise and strong and would save Israel. The people would be happy again and serve God. But then they would forget what God had done and return to idols. This happened many times.

Find It in the Bible
JUDGES 1:1–3:7

DAY 77
DEBORAH JUDGES ISRAEL

O ne of Israel's judges was Deborah. She was the only woman ever to judge Israel. People would come to see her in the hills of Ephraim. Deborah sat under a palm tree giving advice and solving problems. Like the other judges, Deborah had God's Spirit with her. This is why people followed her advice.

But in the north, a Canaanite king named Jabin attacked Israel. Israel had left God and was worshiping idols. Deborah sent for Barak. "The God of Israel commands you to raise an army. He'll let you defeat Jabin's army."

Find It in the Bible
JUDGES 4:1–7

THE BRAVERY OF DEBORAH AND JAEL

Deborah had spoken for the Lord. But Barak said, "I won't go to war unless you go with me."

"I will go with you," said Deborah, "but you didn't trust God, so you won't get the honor of this war. God will give this victory to a woman."

Together, they sent out a call for the men in the north. Ten thousand men joined them at Mount Tabor. But this was a small army compared to the Canaanites.

Deborah sent Barak and his army to attack. The Canaanites had no time to get ready. They were frightened and ran away. Chariots, men, and horses all trampled one another. The Lord made a river flood, and many enemies were drowned there.

Sisera, the Canaanite general, jumped from his chariot and ran away. He came to the tent of a woman named Jael. She knew Sisera and invited him in and hid him under a rug. The battle had made him so tired that Sisera fell asleep. Then Jael drove a tent peg into Sisera's head and killed him.

So Deborah and Jael were brave enough to set Israel free.

Find It in the Bible
JUDGES 4:8–24

GIDEON MEETS GOD

The people of Israel turned to evil again. So the Lord made them suffer for leaving him. For seven years, the Midianites raided the land. They took the harvest away so Israel had no food. The people ran from their towns and farms to hide in caves. They cried out to God.

One day a man named Gideon was threshing wheat in a hidden place. Looking up, he saw an angel sitting by an oak tree. "You're a mighty warrior, Gideon," the angel said. "The Lord is with you. Go and save Israel from Midian."

"But, sir, my family is the weakest in my tribe. I am the youngest of my family. How can I save Israel?"

"I will be with you. I will help you drive out the Midianites."

Then Gideon knew that he was talking with God. He brought food for an offering and set it on a rock. The Lord touched it with his staff. Fire leaped up from the rock and consumed the offering. God vanished.

That night, with ten men, Gideon destroyed the image of Baal. He then built an altar and burned an offering to the Lord.

Find It in the Bible
Judges 6:1–32

THE SIGN OF GIDEON'S FLEECE

The Lord's Spirit came upon Gideon. He sounded a trumpet and sent men to the tribes of Israel. "Come help us drive out the Midianites," they called. And Israel sent warriors to Gideon.

The Midianites came against Gideon with a mighty army. From the slopes of Mount Gilboa, Gideon looked down on Midian's camp.

"O Lord God," Gideon prayed, "will you use me to save Israel? I'm going to lay a fleece of wool on the threshing floor. Give me this sign: Tomorrow, dew will be on the fleece but not on the ground. Then I'll know that we'll defeat the Midianites." The next morning, the fleece was dripping with dew. The ground around it was dry.

"O Lord, don't be angry with me," Gideon said. "But give me one more sign. Tomorrow morning make the fleece dry and the ground wet with dew. Then I'll have no doubt." The next morning, the ground was wet and the fleece was dry.

So Gideon and his troops rose early and camped by the spring at Harod. The Midianites camped north in the valley of Jezreel.

Find It in the Bible
JUDGES 6:33–7:1

GIDEON'S TINY ARMY

The Lord told Gideon, "Your army is too large. People will say, 'We won the victory by our own power.' Send home those who are afraid." Twenty-two thousand went away. Ten thousand stayed to fight.

Then the Lord said, "There are still too many troops. Take them to drink at the spring. Some will lap the water with their tongues. Others will kneel and scoop water with their hands."

Three hundred men lapped up the water. The rest scooped the water. "I'll use the three hundred that lapped to defeat Midian," God said. "The others may leave."

That night God told him, "Go to the enemy camp. You'll hear what they're saying. This will help you in the fight."

At Midian's enormous camp, Gideon heard a soldier tell another his dream. "I dreamed a loaf of bread tumbled into our camp. It hit the tent and knocked it down." Then the other said, "This is the sword of Gideon. God has given us all to him."

Gideon was glad to hear that Midian was afraid. He thanked God, returned to camp, and prepared for battle.

Find It in the Bible
JUDGES 7:2–15

GIDEON'S VICTORY OVER MIDIAN

Gideon divided his army into three parts. Each soldier held a trumpet and a clay jar with a lamp hidden inside. Silently, they moved down the mountain in the night. At the edge of the camp, they blew their trumpets. Then came the sound of their clay jars breaking. The lamps flashed their light. The soldiers shouted, "The sword of the Lord and of Gideon!"

All three hundred men stood in place around the enemy camp. The soldiers in the camp cried out and fled away. The Midianites began to fight among themselves. They were killing each other.

Gideon called out the men of the nearby tribes. They chased the Midianites. The tribe of Ephraim stopped Midian at the Jordan River. There Midian's princes, Oreb and Zeeb, were killed. Midian never attacked Israel again.

Israel had peace for forty years while Gideon was its judge. The people wanted to make Gideon their king. But Gideon said, "No, the Lord God is the king of Israel. No one but God will rule these tribes."

There were, at different times, fifteen judges over Israel. But of them all, Gideon had the most wisdom, courage, and faith.

Find It in the Bible
JUDGES 7:16–8:32

JEPHTHAH'S FOOLISH PROMISE

When Gideon died, Israel worshiped idols again. The Ammonites made war with them. This was the sixth time Israel was oppressed. Jephthah was the man who set them free.

Before he went into battle, Jephthah made a foolish promise. "God, give me victory. Then I will sacrifice whoever greets me when I get home."

God gave Jephthah a great victory over Ammon. When he returned, his only child ran out to meet him. Jephthah cried out, "O my daughter! I must keep my promise."

His daughter mourned for two months; then Jephthah kept his promise.

Find It in the Bible
JUDGES 11:1–40

THE STRONGMAN SAMSON

In time, Israel began to worship idols again. So God gave them over to their enemies. These enemies were the Philistines. They worshiped an idol called Dagon. This god had a fish's head on a man's body.

The Philistines took all the Israelites' swords and spears so they couldn't fight. They robbed Israel of their crops, so they starved. The people cried to God, and God heard them.

Among the tribe of Dan lived a man named Manoah. An angel came to Manoah's wife and said, "You will have a son. When he grows up, he will save Israel from the Philistines. But your son must never drink any wine. His hair must grow long—he'll be a Nazarite priest.

The child was born and named Samson. He became the strongest man mentioned in the Bible. He didn't lead an army in war like Gideon. The things he did to set his people free he did alone.

Samson met a Philistine woman in Timnah. "I want her for my wife," he told his father. This didn't make Samson's parents happy. But they didn't know God would use this marriage. It would help free Israel from the Philistines.

Find It in the Bible
Judges 13:2–14:4

THE HONEY-FILLED LION

Samson went down to Timnah. As he was passing through a vineyard, a lion roared at him. Then the Lord's Spirit came upon Samson. He tore the lion apart with his bare hands. He went on his way and told no one of the lion.

Later, Samson went to Timnah for his wedding. He stopped to look at the dead lion. It was filled with bees and honey. He scooped out some honey and ate it as he walked. Samson gave some honey to his parents. He didn't tell them it had come from the dead lion.

Find It in the Bible
JUDGES 14:5–9

THE RIDDLE AT THE WEDDING

Samson's wedding feast lasted a whole week. There, the young Philistines enjoyed telling riddles. "I have a riddle," said Samson. "If you answer it, I'll give you thirty suits of clothing. If not, you give me thirty suits of clothing."

They agreed. "Tell us your riddle." Samson told them this riddle:

Out of the eater came something to eat.
Out of the strong came something sweet.

The Philistines didn't know the answer. At last, they went to Samson's wife. "Learn from Samson the riddle's answer. If you don't, we'll burn you up in your family's house."

"Samson, if you love me you'll explain the riddle," his wife pleaded and cried. Because she nagged him, he told her about the lion and honey. Samson's wife told the Philistines. Samson had to bring them thirty suits of clothes.

The Lord's Spirit came upon Samson. He killed thirty Philistines and took their clothes. Samson was so angry that he left his wife and came home to live.

Find It in the Bible
JUDGES 14:10–20

A THOUSAND KILLED WITH A JAWBONE

Soon Samson went to live under a split rock called Etam. The Philistine army attacked the tribe of Judah. "What do you want from us?" Judah asked.

"We have come to bind and kill Samson," they answered.

Then three thousand men of Judah went to see Samson. "Why did you kill the Philistines?" they asked. "We suffer for what you do." So, tying Samson with new ropes, they took him away. The Philistines shouted joyfully when they saw Samson brought to them. But they didn't know what he was about to do. Samson broke the new ropes as if they were string. He grabbed a mule's jawbone and started swinging. That day, Samson killed a thousand Philistines. Afterwards, he was so thirsty he was about to die. He called out to God and water sprang up from the ground.

Samson fell in love with another Philistine woman. The name of this woman was Delilah. The Philistine rulers wanted to stop Samson more than ever. They came to Delilah. "Find out what makes Samson so strong. If you help us, we'll give you 1,100 pieces of silver."

Find It in the Bible
JUDGES 15:9–16:5

DAY 88
THE STRONGMAN'S SECRET

Three times Delilah begged Samson, "Tell me the secret of your strength." Each time, the Philistines couldn't hold him.

"Tie me with fresh bowstrings," Samson said. But he broke them like burning string.

"Tie me with new ropes. Then I'll lose my strength." But he broke these ropes like thread.

"Weave my hair into your loom like cloth. Then I'll be like everyone else." While Samson slept, Delilah wove. But when the Philistines tried to capture him, Samson broke the loom.

"How can you tell me you love me?" Delilah cried. "You've lied to me."

Find It in the Bible
JUDGES 16:6–15

SAMSON'S STRENGTH IS LOST

Samson was tired of Delilah's pleading and nagging. Day after day, she begged him for the secret of his strength. So he finally told her the mystery. "My hair has never been cut," he said. "I've been a Nazarite priest for God since my birth. If my hair was cut, my Nazarite vow would be broken. God would leave me and so would my great strength."

Delilah smiled. At last she had the secret. The Philistine chiefs came with money in their hands. That night Samson slept with his head in her lap. He was sound asleep. The Philistines quietly cut off Samson's long hair. He began to weaken and all his strength left. Then Delilah shouted, "Wake up, Samson! The Philistines are after you!"

Samson jumped up, thinking, "This is like the other times. I'll shake them off." He didn't know that the Lord had left him. His hair was cut and his vow was broken. The Philistines easily took Samson prisoner and gouged out his eyes.

They took him down to Gaza. Locked in bronze shackles, Samson turned the grindstone in their mill. But slowly his hair began to grow long again.

Find It in the Bible
JUDGES 16:16–22

THE DEATH OF SAMSON

O ur god, Dagon, has given us Samson!" the Philistines shouted, feasting. Dagon's temple was filled with three thousand men, women, and children. "Bring in Samson to entertain us," they said and laughed.

Samson came, performed, and rested against the temple's pillars. There he prayed: "O God, remember me and strengthen me. Let me pay them back for my eyes." He then leaned his weight against the pillars. "Let me die with the Philistines," he said, pushing powerfully. The temple fell on the feasting Philistines.

Samson killed more Philistines in his death that he had in all his life.

Find It in the Bible
JUDGES 16:23–31

RUTH JOINS NAOMI

A famine came to the land when the judges ruled Israel. Elimelech of Bethlehem moved his family to Moab. After ten years there, Elimelech died. His two sons were married to women of Moab. But then they died, too. So Elimelech's wife, Naomi, and her daughters-in-law were widows.

Naomi heard that God had brought good harvests to Israel. She decided to return. She told each of her sons' wives, "Return to your mother's home. May God be kind to you and give you a new husband." She kissed them both and they wept together.

One young widow, Orpah, did go back to her family. But the second, Ruth, wouldn't leave Naomi. "See," said Naomi, "Orpah has returned to her people and her gods. You go, too."

"Don't make me leave you or stop following you," Ruth said. "Where you go, I'll go. Where you live, I'll live. Your people will be my people, and your God, my God. Where you die, I'll die, and there I'll be buried. Only death will come between us."

Naomi saw that Ruth was firm. She said no more, and they returned together to Bethlehem.

Find It in the Bible
Ruth 1:1–22

RUTH MEETS BOAZ

The time of barley harvest had come to Bethlehem. When they harvested their fields, the Israelites always left some grain standing. This grain was left for the poor and gleaned, or gathered, later.

Ruth went out to glean in the fields of a man named Boaz. He was of the family of Elimelech, Naomi's dead husband. Boaz was watching the harvest and saw Ruth. "Who is the young woman gleaning in the field?" he asked the workers.

"She came back with Naomi from Moab," they answered. Boaz gave Ruth water and urged her to stay in his field.

Find It in the Bible
RUTH 2:1–9

RUTH—THE MOTHER OF KINGS

I've heard you left Moab to come here with Naomi," Boaz said to Ruth. "You have come under the Lord's wings. May he reward you." Boaz gave Ruth food for her lunch and spoke to the harvesters. "Be kind to her. Leave plenty of grain for her gleanings."

That night Ruth showed Naomi all her gleanings. She told Naomi of the kind rich man. "He is a relative of mine," Naomi told her. "Stay in his field until the harvest ends." So Ruth continued to glean the fields of Boaz.

The harvest ended. Boaz held a feast on his threshing floor. After the feast Ruth went to Boaz. Naomi had told her that this was the thing to do. Ruth respectfully spoke. "You are a part of my husband's family. His father was Elimelech. Please be kind to me and to Naomi for their sake." Israel's law said that Boaz could take Ruth into his family.

Boaz soon fell in love with Ruth, and they were married. They named their son Obed. Their grandson was Jesse, the father of David, the king of Israel.

This is how Ruth, the widow of Moab, became the mother of Israel's kings.

Find It in the Bible
RUTH 2:10–4:22

SAMUEL STAYS IN GOD'S HOUSE

There was once a priest and judge of Israel named Eli. He and his sons served God in the tabernacle at Shiloh. Every year a man named Elkanah and his family worshiped there. Like many men in those days, Elkanah had two wives. One had children. The other, named Hannah, did not. Hannah often cried because she couldn't have children.

One year at Shiloh, Eli saw Hannah praying outside the tabernacle. "O Lord," she said, "look how sad I am. Remember me and allow me to have a little boy. I will give him to you as a Nazarite priest."

The Lord heard Hannah's prayer and gave her a baby boy. She named him Samuel, which means "asked of God." When Samuel was still a little child, she brought him to Eli. Hannah said to the priest, "I asked God for this boy. I promised him to the Lord for all his life. Let him stay here with you and grow up in God's house."

So little Samuel stayed in Shiloh, helping Eli, the old priest. Eli's own sons were priests, but they were also scoundrels. So Samuel was a comfort to Eli.

Find It in the Bible
1 SAMUEL 1:1–2:25

GOD CALLS SAMUEL

One night, Samuel lay resting in the tabernacle. The Lord called to him, "Samuel, Samuel."

"Here I am!" said Samuel, and he ran to Eli's room. "Did you call me?"

"No," Eli answered. "Go back to bed, my son."

The same thing happened a second time. Samuel didn't know God then, or God's words. Then Samuel was called a third time. At last, Eli understood that the Lord was calling the boy. Eli then told Samuel how to answer.

The Lord came and stood there calling as before. Samuel answered "Speak, Lord, for your servant is listening."

Find It in the Bible
1 SAMUEL 3:1–10

A CURSE ON ELI'S HOUSE

That night, God told Samuel what was about to happen to Eli's family. "I am going to take action in Israel," the Lord said. "Later, when people hear of it, their ears will tingle."

"I am about to punish Eli's family forever. Eli knows about his sons' wickedness. They are a curse to me and steal my sacrifices. But Eli does nothing, so the sins of Eli's house will never be washed away."

Samuel lay there until morning. Then he got up and opened the doors to the Lord's house. But he was afraid to tell Eli what God had said to him.

"Samuel, my son," Eli called.

"Here I am."

"What did the Lord tell you last night? Don't hide anything from me." So Samuel told Eli everything he had heard. "This is the Lord," Eli said. "May he do what seems good to him."

As Samuel grew, the Lord was with him. Everything he said had meaning. All the tribes of Israel knew of Samuel. "He is a prophet who can be trusted," they said.

Find It in the Bible
1 SAMUEL 3:11–21

GOD'S ARK IS LOST

Old and blind, Eli was still high priest and judge. In those days the Philistines made war with Israel. Over four thousand men were killed in Israel's defeat.

"Why did the Lord let the Philistines win?" Israel's chiefs didn't know about Eli's curse. "Let's bring God's ark of the covenant from Shiloh," they decided. "With it, God will be among us and will save us."

Eli's two sons were priests in Shiloh. Their job was to care for the ark of the covenant. But instead, they let the warriors take it into battle.

Israel's army shouted for joy. God's ark had come into their camp. But when the battle came, thirty thousand Israeli soldiers were killed. The ark was captured by the Philistines. Eli's sons were killed in the fight.

Sitting by the gate in Shiloh, Eli waited. He was worried sick about the ark. A man raced from the battle with the news: "Your sons are dead. The ark is captured." Hearing this, Eli fell over backward. His neck was broken and he died. Because the ark was captured, God's glory left Israel.

Find It in the Bible
1 SAMUEL 4:1–22

ISRAEL ASKS FOR A KING

After seven months, the Philistines returned the ark of the covenant. Samuel judged Israel in peace. The people broke their idols and served the Lord. But the twelve tribes wanted a king.

"You're growing old and your sons cannot rule well," they said. "Choose a king for us like the nations have."

Samuel wasn't happy. He was afraid a king would turn Israel from God. But God said, "Do what they want, Samuel. They're not leaving you but me and have been ever since coming out of Egypt."

"A king will take your sons away to be servants and soldiers," Samuel said. "They'll do his farming and build weapons for war. He'll take your best farms for his friends. Your daughters will cook and serve in his palace. The best flocks will be his, and you'll be his slaves. A king will make you weep and cry."

The elders refused his advice. "We want to be like the nations," they replied. "Give us a king to rule us and lead us into battle."

God said to Samuel, "Give them a king." So Samuel sent them away.

Find It in the Bible
1 SAMUEL 8:1–22

GOD CHOOSES ISRAEL'S KING

Saul, a wealthy Benjamite, was a tall, handsome young man. Saul and a servant were near Zuph searching for stray donkeys. The servant said, "A prophet lives in this town. He may know where the donkeys are."

The day before, the Lord had spoken to Samuel. "Tomorrow, a man will come from Benjamin. Make him the king of Israel. He'll save my people from the Philistines." When Samuel saw Saul walking up the hill, God spoke again. "This is the man I told you about yesterday."

Saul asked Samuel, "Where does the prophet live?"

"I'm the prophet," Samuel replied. "Come with me, and we'll eat together. And don't worry about the donkeys. They've been found. Do you know that Israel hopes in you and your father's house?"

"I'm from Benjamin," Saul replied. "That's the smallest tribe in Israel. My family is the smallest in Benjamin. Why do you talk to me like this?"

But Samuel brought Saul to the feast. He was given the best seat. His food was the finest of all that was served.

Find It in the Bible
1 SAMUEL 9:1–25

DAY 100
SAMUEL ANOINTS ISRAEL'S KING

In the morning, Samuel walked with Saul from the town. Sending the servant ahead, Samuel told Saul, "God has told me to anoint you king to rule over Israel." He then poured olive oil from a small bottle onto Saul's head.

"This is how you'll know it's true: As you travel, you'll come to Rachel's tomb. There two men will say, 'Your donkeys have been found. Now your father is looking for you.'" And so it happened.

After three hundred years under the judges, Israel had its own king.

Find It in the Bible
1 SAMUEL 9:26–10:27

SAMUEL GIVES THE KINGDOM TO SAUL

A month had passed since Saul was anointed king. In the meantime, the Ammonites attacked Israel at Jabesh. The news spread, and Israel wept. Saul heard the weeping as he worked with his oxen. "What's the matter?" he asked. "Why are people crying?" Saul was told of the attack at Jabesh.

When Saul heard this, God's Spirit came on him. Anger burned in him like fire. Quickly, he cut his oxen into pieces and sent them around Israel. This was Saul's message: "Join me to fight the Ammonites. If you don't, this will happen to your oxen."

Over three hundred thousand soldiers joined Saul to scatter the Ammonites. Samuel saw Saul's victory. "Let's go to Gilgal," Samuel told the people. "There we can set up the kingdom again." Gilgal was where Joshua had first camped in Canaan.

There Samuel gave the kingdom to Saul. He offered sacrifices to God and said farewell to the people and recounted their history. "I'll always pray for you," Samuel said. "Serve the Lord faithfully. Don't be wicked again. If you are, you and your king will be swept away."

Find It in the Bible
1 SAMUEL 11:1–12:25

DAY 102
SAUL OFFERS A SACRIFICE

The people hoped Saul would defeat the Philistines. But after two years, the Philistines had grown stronger. Saul's army did overrun a Philistine fort at Geba. But this caused the Philistines to send horsemen and chariots. There were so many soldiers, they looked like sand by the sea. Saul blew a trumpet, calling the Israelites to war. Many came, but they came in fear.

Saul waited seven days. Samuel was to come and offer a sacrifice before the battle. But he didn't arrive on time. Saul didn't see how he could wait any longer. Many in his army were leaving. So Saul himself burned the offering to God. Just then Samuel reached the camp. "What have you done?" he asked.

"My men were scattering," Saul answered. "I thought the enemy might attack. So I made the offering myself."

"You have done wrong and not kept the Lord's commands," said Samuel. "If you had obeyed and trusted God, you'd be safe. But now God will find some other man to fulfill his will. This will be a man seeking the Lord's heart. Someday, God will take the kingdom from you and give it to him."

Find It in the Bible
1 SAMUEL 13:1-14

GOD RIPS AWAY THE KINGDOM

Saul defeated the Philistines. He also drove back all of Israel's enemies. Finally, Israel had peace.

But there was one more tribe to fight. God wanted the Amalekites totally destroyed. Saul's army demolished their city but saved the animals for sacrifices. Samuel heard of this. He told Saul, "God wants your obedience more than your sacrifices. He has rejected you as king." As Samuel turned to leave, Saul grabbed and ripped his robe. Then Samuel spoke to Saul for the last time: "Today God has ripped your kingdom from you and given it to a better man."

Find It in the Bible
1 SAMUEL 15:1–35

DAVID—THE ANOINTED BOY

God spoke to Samuel again: "Bring oil to Bethlehem. There you'll anoint Jesse's son as the new king."

At Bethlehem, Samuel offered God a sacrifice. Jesse and his seven sons were there. Samuel thought, "I'll anoint one of these young men." But God said, "They are good looking, but I don't want them. People only see what others look like. But I look at their heart."

"Do you have another son?" asked Samuel.

"My youngest son, David, is with the sheep."

Jesse sent for David. When the boy arrived God said, "Anoint him. This is the one."

Find It in the Bible
1 SAMUEL 16:1–12

DAVID—THE MUSICIAN-KING

David was only about fifteen, with bright eyes and rosy cheeks. Samuel anointed him with oil as his older brothers watched. God's Spirit was with David from that day on. At the same time, Saul became very gloomy. He was not at peace with God.

Because David played the harp well, Jesse sent him to Saul. Saul's servants thought that the music would help cheer the king. Saul loved David. His music made the king feel better. But Saul didn't know that Samuel had anointed David. The boy who played the harp for Saul was Israel's future king.

Find It in the Bible
1 SAMUEL 16:13–23

DAY 106
DAVID—THE SHEPHERD-WARRIOR

While Saul was king, the Philistines battled with Israel. There was a giant Philistine named Goliath. He was nine feet tall and impossible to fight. He dared any Israeli to fight him. "Let him kill me!" Goliath roared. "Then we'll be your servants." But Saul's army was afraid.

"Who's this?" David asked. "Don't let him defy God's army." With his shepherd's staff in hand, David went to fight Goliath. From a stream, David picked five stones for his slingshot.

David challenged Goliath: "You come with a sword. I come in the name of the Lord of Hosts."

Find It in the Bible
1 SAMUEL 17:1–45

DAVID—THE GIANT-KILLER

Goliath saw David carrying a shepherd's staff. "You're here to fight me with a stick?" Goliath cursed. "Do you think I'm a dog?"

"Today, God will give me your life!" David shouted. "I'll strike you down and cut off your head. The birds and animals will feast on the Philistine army. The earth will know there's a God in Israel."

Then, running at Goliath, David put a stone in his slingshot. He hurled the stone deep into the giant's forehead. Goliath fell dead to the ground. That day, David won a great victory for Israel.

Find It in the Bible
1 SAMUEL 17:46–52

DAVID—KING ON THE RUN

David came to Saul's tent, holding Goliath's head. Saul wouldn't let David return to his father's house. Instead, David became a leader in Saul's army. His best friend was Saul's son, Jonathan.

David was a winner in whatever he did. Everyone, even Saul's servants, were happy with him. One day Saul's army was returning from war. Women met them, dancing and singing:

> *Saul has killed his thousands,*
> *and David has killed his ten thousands.*

This made Saul very angry and jealous. He wanted David dead. In time, David had to jump from his window to escape from Saul.

As they ran from Saul, David and his men were hungry. At the tabernacle, they were given the bread from the holy place. Goliath's sword was there. So David took it for his own and hurried on. They finally hid in the caves of Adullam in Judah. Four hundred poor and troubled men joined David there. He was their captain.

David stayed in hiding until Saul died.

Find It in the Bible
1 SAMUEL 17:57–22:5

DAVID SPARES SAUL'S LIFE

David ran to the Rocks of the Wild Goats. He hid from Saul in a dark cave. Saul came alone and rested there. "Here's your chance," David's men whispered. "Kill your enemy."

"I won't harm God's anointed king," David said. Instead, he crept out and cut the corner from Saul's cloak.

Saul awoke. As he walked away, David called, "My lord the king." He waved the piece of cloak. "This proves that I don't want to hurt you."

And Saul began to cry. "May the Lord reward you with good. Now I know that you will be king of Israel."

Find It in the Bible
1 SAMUEL 24:1–22

SAUL SEEKS SAMUEL'S SPIRIT

Years passed, Samuel died, and Saul was old, sick, and alone. The Philistines gathered a huge army to fight against Israel. Saul was afraid and had no idea of what to do. He asked the Lord but got no answer. Saul learned that a psychic lived at Endor. She claimed to contact people who were dead. Saul wore a disguise and went to Endor at night.

"Bring back the spirit of Samuel," Saul said.

The psychic replied, "I see an old man wrapped in a robe coming up from the ground."

God allowed Samuel's spirit to speak to Saul. "Why have you disturbed my rest?" he said.

"What shall I do? The Philistines are at war and God won't answer me."

"I told you that God has ripped the kingdom from you. Tomorrow you and your sons will be in death with me."

The next day, there was a huge battle on Mount Gilboa. Two days later David got the news: "Saul and his sons are dead; the battle is lost." David and his men wept for Saul and Jonathan and Israel's soldiers.

Saul had been king in Israel for almost fifteen years.

Find It in the Bible
1 SAMUEL 28:3–19, 31:1–12, 2 SAMUEL 1:1–27

DAVID—THE CONQUERING KING

Saul was dead, but David didn't become king. Some people wanted the king to come from Saul's family. Seven years passed. Israel still didn't have its true king. David was thirty years old when Israel finally made him king.

Again, the Philistines raised an army against Israel. They camped in the valley of Rephaim while David prayed. "Go around behind them," God answered. "You'll hear marching in the tree tops. This means I've gone into battle ahead of you. I'll strike down the Philistine's army." That day, David conquered the Philistines after one hundred years of war.

Find It in the Bible
2 SAMUEL 5:1–25

DAVID—THE JOYFUL DANCER

The ark of the covenant had been hidden away while Saul ruled. David decided it was time to bring it to Jerusalem. A new oxcart was built just to carry the ark. As it rolled toward Jerusalem, David and other Israelis followed behind. They sang and made music and danced with all their strength.

The tabernacle was set up on Mount Zion. The priests carried the ark into the tent of meeting and offerings were burned to the Lord. Israel was shouting with joy, and David used all his strength dancing before the Lord.

Find It in the Bible
2 Samuel 6:1–23

DAY 113
DAVID'S HEART FOR GOD

Jerusalem became known as the City of David. There the priests offered sacrifices to God every day at the tabernacle. For a long time God had not been properly worshiped. But now these services were held in Jerusalem. David lived in a beautiful cedar house on Mount Zion. One day he spoke to the prophet Nathan: "Look at this. I live in a cedar house. But God's ark is still in a tent."

That night the Lord spoke to Nathan: "I brought Israel out of Egypt. Ever since then my ark has been in the tent of meeting. No one has ever thought of building me a cedar house. But now David has a heart to build my house. Tell my servant David, 'I took you from the sheep pasture. There you followed the sheep. I made you prince over my people Israel. I gave you a great name and great power. Now I will give you a kingdom. Your son will sit on the throne after you die. He will build a house for me. You and your children and their families will have the kingdom. It will last forever.' "

Find It in the Bible
2 SAMUEL 7:1–29

THE DEATH OF URIAH

When David first became king, he went into battle with his army. Later, he stayed in his palace while the army went to fight.

One evening, David was walking on the roof of his palace. He looked into a nearby garden and saw a beautiful woman. "Who is this woman?" he asked his servant.

"Her name is Bathsheba. She's the wife of Uriah."

Uriah was away fighting in David's army. David sent for Uriah's wife and spoke with her. He loved her and wanted her to be his wife. But Bathsheba was married to Uriah.

David made a wicked plan. He wrote to Joab, the general of Israel's army. "Send Uriah to the front of the battle," David wrote. "Leave him there in the hard fighting. Then Uriah will be killed."

Joab followed David's orders. He sent Uriah to fight near the city walls. There Uriah was killed.

Bathsheba mourned for her dead husband for some time. Then David sent for her. He brought Bathsheba into his house and married her. A baby was born to them. David loved the child. But God disliked what David had done to Uriah.

Find It in the Bible
2 SAMUEL 11:1–27

DAY 115
"YOU ARE THE MAN!"

The Lord sent Nathan the prophet to David. He told this story: "There were two men—one rich, the other poor. The poor man had one lamb. It grew up in his home with his children. One day, the rich man had a visitor for dinner. But he didn't serve his own meat. He robbed the poor man and killed his lamb for food."

"That man should die!" said David.

"You are the man!" said Nathan. "God made you king. You have everything, but you killed Uriah. You, your wives, and your children will suffer for this."

Find It in the Bible
2 SAMUEL 12:1–14

A DEATH AND A BIRTH

Nathan's rebuke shocked and saddened David. "I've sinned against the Lord," he said.

"The Lord forgives you," Nathan replied. "You won't die. But Bathsheba's child will die because of what you did."

The baby was sick for six days. David wouldn't eat or sleep. All he did was pray to God for the child. On the seventh day, Bathsheba's baby died. When the king learned about the death, he washed and dressed. "While my child was still alive I didn't eat; I only wept," David said. " 'Who knows,' I thought, 'maybe God will save the child.' But now he is dead; why should I cry? Can I bring him back again? I will go to be with him someday. But he will never return to me."

Bathsheba and David had another baby boy. David named him Solomon. Nathan the prophet named him Jedidiah, which means "loved by God."

Nathan had predicted that suffering would come to David because of Uriah. Soon this began to happen. Many of David's sons grew up wild and wicked. One was David's oldest son, Absalom, a handsome man with beautiful long hair.

Find It in the Bible
2 Samuel 12:13–24

DAVID—ON THE RUN AGAIN

David's beautiful son Absalom became very angry at Amnon. They were half brothers, both sons of David. Amnon had been cruel to Absalom's sister, Tamar. Absalom hid his anger until the day he gave a feast. All of David's sons were there, including Amnon. While they were feasting, Absalom's servants rushed in and killed Amnon. The others ran for their lives back to David. While they were still on the way, David heard the news. But he was told that all his sons were killed. He tore his clothes and mourned. Absalom ran the other way and hid with his grandparents.

David mourned for Amnon. But he loved Absalom, and after three years, his son returned. Absalom wanted to be king and become powerful in Israel. One day, Absalom gathered his followers at Hebron as if to worship. Instead, he had himself declared king of Israel.

"Absalom is loved by everyone in Israel." This report alarmed David.

"Get up!" he said. "Let's run, or we'll never escape from Absalom." So the king and his household made their getaway. People cried when they saw their king flee into the desert.

Find It in the Bible
2 SAMUEL 13:1–15:23

THE DEATH OF ABSALOM

East of the Jordan River is Gilead. It's a high place where David could safely hide. There an army gathered around the king. It was not big like Absalom's army, but it was brave. As his army marched out to battle, David said, "Be gentle with Absalom."

The armies fought a terrible battle. Twenty thousand men died. The armies scattered into the forest. Absalom saw his defeat coming and rode away to escape. Suddenly, his hair caught the branches of an oak tree. He was left hanging in the tree.

Three spears were in Joab's hands when he found Absalom. These pierced through the heart of David's son. Absalom was cut from the tree and thrown dead in a pit. Over the pit they built a huge heap of stones.

Watching by the city gates, David could see a runner. "This is the messenger from the battle," he said. The runner approached. David asked, "Is Absalom all right?"

"All your enemies should lie dead like him."

"O my son Absalom," David cried. "I wish I had died instead of you. My son! My son!"

Find It in the Bible
2 SAMUEL 17:24–18:33

THE SADNESS OF DAVID

The king's army heard that David wasn't rejoicing about Absalom's death. The great victory turned into sorrow and sadness for the soldiers. David hid his face. "O my son Absalom, O Absalom, my son, my son!"

Joab told him, "This army has saved your life. Your sons and daughters and wives are all safe. You act like you love the one who hated you. Do you hate the ones who love you? Speak kindly to your army. If you don't, I'm sure disaster will come to you."

So David went out and spoke kind words to his troops.

Find It in the Bible
2 SAMUEL 19:1–8

THE PLACE OF GOD'S HOUSE

David ruled a spacious, peaceful kingdom in Israel. His lands stretched from the Euphrates to the border of Egypt. On the west was the Great Sea. On the east, the great desert. Then David did a sinful thing. "Go through the tribes of Israel," he ordered Joab. "Count the people so I may know how many there are."

Joab knew this was wrong. But he had to obey his king. The Lord disliked what David had done. So he sent a disease on the land for three days. Seventy thousand people died. A destroying angel stood at Ornan's threshing floor ready to destroy Jerusalem. But God said, "Enough! Do no more." So the angel ordered David to offer a sacrifice there. Ornan threshed at the top of Mount Moriah.

Ornan offered his land, oxen, and tools for no cost. Instead, David paid the full price. There, where Abraham had offered Isaac so long before, David sacrificed. He called upon the Lord, and God answered him with fire. He burned the oxen with the threshing tools on the altar.

Then David said, "This is the place we'll build God's house. Israel's altar for burnt offering will be here."

Find It in the Bible
2 Samuel 24:1–25; 1 Chronicles 21:1–27

PREPARING FOR GOD'S HOUSE

David had found the place to build God's house. In his heart, David wanted to do the building. But God said, "You've been a man of war. In many battles you've killed many men. My house will be built by a peaceful man. When you die, your son Solomon will be king. There will be peace, and he'll build my house."

So David gathered all the materials for the building. He made everything ready for God's temple to be built on Mount Moriah. "Solomon," he said, "God promised peace while you are king. He'll be with you, and you'll build his house."

David grew old. One day Bathsheba came to him. "King David," she said, "you promised that Solomon would be the next king. But Absalom's brother Adonijah is now preparing to become king."

"Bathsheba," David answered, "I promise that your son Solomon will sit on my throne. Make everything ready. Today, I make Solomon king."

Solomon became king and the people rejoiced. Adonijah heard the sound of singing and cheering. It shook the ground. He was afraid Solomon would kill him. "Go home, Adonijah," said King Solomon. "If you are honorable, you will live."

Find It in the Bible
1 KINGS 1:1–53; 1 CHRONICLES 22:1–19

SOLOMON PRAYS FOR WISDOM

David ruled Israel for thirty-three years. Then he died and was buried in Jerusalem. Solomon sat as king on David's throne and his kingdom was strong. Israel was at peace.

Before the temple was built, an altar stood at Gibeon, north of Jerusalem. Solomon prayed there and offered a thousand sacrifices. One night the Lord came to Solomon in a dream. "What would you like me to give you?" God asked.

Solomon said, "I am only a young man, Lord. I don't know how to rule this great people. Give me wisdom and knowledge to know right and wrong."

The Lord was pleased that Solomon had asked this. "You didn't ask for a long life," God said. "Nor did you ask for riches, victory, or power. Instead you've asked for wisdom to judge my people. So I give you greater wisdom than any other king. No other ruler will ever have more wisdom than you. And because you've asked only for this, I'll give you more. You'll have riches and honor. No other ruler will compare to you. Obey my words like your father David obeyed. Then you'll have a long life and rule for many years."

Find It in the Bible
1 Kings 3:3–15

THE WISDOM OF SOLOMON

Solomon could build God's great temple. He could also wisely judge small matters. One day two women came with one baby. "Her baby died and she switched it for mine," said the first.

"No, the dead baby is yours," the other argued.

"My son is living," said the first. They squabbled in front of the king.

"Bring a sword," commanded Solomon. "Divide this baby. Each can have half."

"Give her the child!" The first woman loved the boy. "Don't kill my son."

"This is the true mother," Solomon decided. And Israel was in awe of him.

Find It in the Bible
1 KINGS 3:16–28

GOD'S TEMPLE IS BUILT

The most important thing Solomon did was build God's temple. It stood on Mount Moriah in Jerusalem.

The stones of the temple walls were cut to fit perfectly. The cedar posts and beams were carved and then brought to Jerusalem. So while the temple was built there was very little noise. It was designed much like the tabernacle only much larger. Also the temple was not a tent. It was strongly built of stone and cedarwood.

In seven years, the temple was complete. The ark was placed in the holy of holies. Solomon and the people worshiped there.

Find It in the Bible
1 KINGS 5:1–8:66

THE KINGDOM OF SOLOMON
PART ONE

One night after the temple was finished, the Lord appeared to Solomon. "I've heard your prayer," God said, "and I have made this house holy. It will be my house, and I will dwell there.

"Walk with me like your father David did. Do the things I want. Then your kingdom will last forever. But if you stop following me, I'll leave this house. I'll let Israel's enemies destroy the temple you've built for me."

Israel was greater than ever under King Solomon. Many countries sent their princes to visit Solomon and see his riches. They were amazed at his wisdom and understanding. Some said he was the wisest man in the world. Solomon wrote many of his wise sayings in the book of Proverbs. Others have been lost. It is said that he wrote one thousand songs.

Solomon's palace stood on Mount Moriah below the temple. It had so many cedar pillars that they looked like a forest. It was called "The House of the Forest of Lebanon." From it a wide stone staircase rose up to the temple. Solomon used these stairs when he went up to worship.

Find It in the Bible
1 KINGS 9:1–9

THE QUEEN OF SHEBA

S heba was a land in southern Arabia, a thousand miles from Israel. The queen of Sheba heard of Solomon's wisdom. She came with rich gifts to visit him. While they were together, she asked Solomon many difficult questions. Solomon answered them all. He showed her his glorious palace: his throne, his servants, his food, and the steps up to the temple.

"All I've heard of your wisdom and greatness is true," she said. "The Lord who has set you on Israel's throne is blessed." The queen gave him great treasures and returned to Sheba.

Find It in the Bible
1 KINGS 10:1–13

THE KINGDOM OF SOLOMON
PART TWO

There was a dark side to Solomon's kingdom. All the beautiful buildings and the splendor of his palace cost money. These were paid for by high taxes on the people. Many men worked on buildings and became soldiers. Others worked in Solomon's fields and were servants to him.

Solomon didn't care about the poor people of Israel. Nor did he love God with his whole heart. His queen was the daughter of Egypt's Pharaoh. She lived in a beautiful palace. Solomon had many other wives from foreign countries. Each of them worshiped idols in their homes. To make them happy, Solomon built a temple for idols. Images of false gods stood around Jerusalem. Solomon himself offered sacrifices to them.

All this made the Lord very angry. "I'm going to rip the kingdom from you," God said. "I'll give it to your servant. But not while you live. I'll rip it from the hand of your son. One tribe will be left. Your son will rule it because your father David loved me."

The people cried against Solomon. He had made their lives too hard.

Find It in the Bible
1 KINGS 10:14–11:13

ISRAEL IS DIVIDED

Solomon ruled Israel for forty years. Then he died and was buried in Jerusalem. Solomon's son, Rehoboam, sat as king on David's throne. But he was weak. Jeroboam, who was Rehoboam's rival, led the people. They said to Rehoboam, "Do not be like your father, over-taxing and overworking us, and you can be our king."

Said Rehoboam, "In three days, I will let you know."

Jeroboam and the people waited three days. Rehoboam asked his father's old, wise men what to do.

"Be wise," they advised. "Do what they ask."

Then Rehoboam talked to the young princes of Israel. "How shall I answer the people?" he asked.

"Tell them that you're much stronger than your father," they advised.

On the third day, Jeroboam and the people returned. Rehoboam ignored the old men's advice. He did what the young princes said he should do. That day, ten of Israel's tribes revolted and made Jeroboam their king.

Find It in the Bible
1 KINGS 11:42–12:20

THE SIN OF JEROBOAM

Jeroboam ruled the ten tribes in northern Israel. Rehoboam was king over the tribe of Judah and part of Benjamin. They lived in Jerusalem and southern Israel.

All of Israel, both north and south, worshiped in Jerusalem. "My people still sacrifice in Jerusalem," Jeroboam said. "They may turn back to Rehoboam and kill me." He decided to make two calves of gold. "Here are your gods," he said to Israel. "They rescued you from Egypt." Jeroboam set up one calf on an altar in Bethel. The other he put in Dan. He caused God's people to worship idols. This has been called the Sin of Jeroboam ever since.

Jeroboam was at Bethel worshiping the false god. That day a prophet came from Judah. He cried out, "O altar, altar, the Lord says this: 'A man will come from David's family named Josiah. O altar! He will burn the priests who worship here. Here is the proof: The altar will break down. Its ashes will spill out.' "

In anger, Jeroboam tried to grab the prophet. He reached out. Instantly his hand shriveled up. Just then the altar broke apart and its ashes spilled out.

Find It in the Bible
1 KINGS 12:32–13:5

THE PUNISHMENT OF JEROBOAM

Jeroboam's son, Abijah, became very sick. The king told the boy's mother, "Disguise yourself. No one must know you're my wife. Go to the prophet Ahijah and ask if the child will get well."

The Lord said to Ahijah, "Jeroboam's wife is coming to see you. Tell her what will happen to her son."

"Welcome, wife of Jeroboam," said the prophet. "Tell Jeroboam that the Lord says this: 'I made you the leader of my people. I ripped the kingdom away from David's family for you. But you have done more evil than any other king. I'm very angry because you made false gods. So I'll bring evil to your family. All of your children will die. The family of Jeroboam will disappear like burning trash.'"

Ahijah continued, "Go away to your house, woman. When your feet enter the city, the child will die. Israel will be taken from this good land. They'll be scattered far away because of the Sin of Jeroboam."

Jeroboam ruled twenty-two years in Israel and died. His son Nadab then became king.

Find It in the Bible
1 KINGS 14:1–20

THE HISTORY OF ISRAEL'S KINGS

One of King Nadab's servants was named Baasha. He plotted against Nadab, killed him, and made himself king. As Ahijah prophesied, Baasha killed Jeroboam's family because of Jeroboam's leading Israel to idolatry.

God sent Jehu to prophesy against Baasha: "I lifted you from the dust. I made you Israel's prince. But you've lived like Jeroboam and made Israel sin. I'll make your family just like Jeroboam's. They'll all be destroyed."

When Baasha died, his son Elah became king. Elah's servant Zimri killed him and his family and tried to become king. Instead, Omri and the Israelite army trapped him in his palace. Zimri set it on fire and burned with it. Omri became king.

Like the other kings, Omri worshiped idols. But his kingdom was strong and he made peace with Judah. Omri built the city of Samaria on a hilltop. In the south, Jerusalem was the main city of Judah. In the north, Samaria was the main city of Israel.

After Omri came the worst king of all— Ahab. His wife, Jezebel, hunted God's prophets and killed them.

Find It in the Bible
1 KINGS 15:27–16:33

ELIJAH THE TISHBITE

When Ahab was king, a great prophet came out of Gilead. This was Elijah the Tishbite. He spoke to Ahab: "The God of Israel is living. I'm with him. There will be neither dew nor rain until I say so." Then Elijah went away to the east and hid at Cherith Creek.

"When you're thirsty, drink from the creek," God said. "I've commanded the ravens to feed you when you're hungry." Morning and evening ravens brought Elijah meat and bread. He drank from the creek. But it soon dried up because no rain fell in the land.

Find It in the Bible
1 KINGS 17:1–7

ELIJAH AND THE WIDOW OF ZAREPHATH

Since Elijah had no water, God told him, "Go and live in Zarephath. I've told a widow there to feed you." So Elijah journeyed to Zarephath. He found the widow near the gate gathering firewood.

"Bring me a little water," he asked. As the widow went for water, Elijah called to her again. "Bring me a bit of bread as well."

The widow answered, "I am about to bake bread. Then all my flour and oil will be gone. My son and I will eat it, lie down, and die."

"First make bread for me," Elijah said. "The God of Israel says this: 'Your flour and oil will last until rain comes again.' " The widow believed him. The jar that held her flour was never empty. The jug of oil didn't run out. This happened exactly as Elijah had said it would.

But then the widow's son got sick. His illness became worse and worse until he stopped breathing. "What do you have against me, O man of God?" she cried. "Did you come to remind me of my sin? Are you here to cause my son's death?"

Find It in the Bible
1 KINGS 17:8–18

DAY 134
ELIJAH REVIVES THE DEAD

The widow's child was dead. Elijah carried the boy up to his room. "O Lord," he cried, "have you brought tragedy to this woman by killing her son?" He lay full-length on the boy three times. Elijah cried out, "O Lord my God! Let this child live." The Lord heard Elijah's voice; the child's life came into him again.

Elijah brought him down the stairs. "See, your son is alive."

"Now I know that you're a man of God. You speak the Lord's words in truth."

Find It in the Bible
1 KINGS 17:19–24

THE RAVING PRIESTS OF BAAL

For three years, no rain fell. Then God said to Elijah, "Go visit Ahab. I'll send rain again."

Meanwhile, Obadiah, who was in charge of Ahab's palace, searched for water. On the way, he met Elijah.

"Is that you, Elijah?"

"Yes, it's me," Elijah replied. "Tell Ahab I'm here."

Ahab saw Elijah and said, "Is that the man who's brought this trouble to Israel?"

"You caused this drought, Ahab," Elijah said. "You've left God to worship Baal. Have Baal's 400 priests and the 450 prophets of Asherah come to Mount Carmel."

At the mountain Elijah announced, "You must choose: Follow Baal or the Lord God. Bring two oxen; one for Baal's priests, one for me. We'll cut them up and put them each on an altar. Then you call on your god; I'll call on the Lord. The one who sends fire on the altar will be Israel's God.

Baal's priests put their ox on the altar and called on Baal all morning: "O Baal, answer us."

Elijah laughed. "Maybe your god is asleep or has wandered away somewhere." Baal's priests raved on past noon with no answer.

Find It in the Bible

1 Kings 18:1–29

THE FAITHFUL PROPHET OF GOD

Elijah built an altar of twelve stones. Each stone represented one of Israel's tribes. The ox and firewood were placed on top. He dug a ditch around the altar. Three times Elijah ordered water poured over the altar. Everything was soaking wet and the ditch was filled up.

Elijah prayed: "O God of Abraham, Isaac, and Israel, show them that you are Israel's God. Turn their hearts back to you." Suddenly, fire came out of the sky and burned up the offering.

When the people saw this, they fell down shouting, "The Lord is God!"

Find It in the Bible
1 KINGS 18:30–39

GOD SPEAKS IN THE SILENCE

Elijah's offering burned up, the water evaporated, and he killed Baal's priests. "When Elijah prayed, it rained!" King Ahab exclaimed.

Jezebel sent a message to Elijah: "I'm going to make you like one of Baal's priests."

Elijah ran for his life. "Take my life, Lord," Elijah said wearily. "I'm no better than anyone else." Then he fell asleep under a broom tree. An angel touched him, saying, "Wake up and eat." Nearby was hot bread and cool water. Elijah ate, then traveled forty days to a cave in Mount Horeb.

"O God," he prayed. "Israel has left you, the prophets are dead, and your altars are broken down. I'm here, but they want to kill me."

"Go out on the mountain," said God. "I'm going to pass by."

The wind blew so strong it shattered the rocks. But God wasn't in the wind. Then came an earthquake. God wasn't there. Then fire. God wasn't in the fire. Finally, there was pure silence and God spoke: "There will be seven thousand in Israel who haven't worshiped Baal."

Find It in the Bible
1 KINGS 18:40–19:18

ELISHA AND THE PROPHET'S CAPE

God spoke to Elijah in the silence. "Find Elisha, Shaphat's son. Anoint him to be the prophet in your place. On the way, anoint Hazael in Damascus as king of Syria. Then anoint Jehu, Nimshi's son, as king over Israel. Whoever escapes from Hazael's sword, Jehu will kill. Whoever escapes Jehu's sword, Elisha will kill. Despite these deaths, seven thousand will be left who haven't worshiped Baal. These people haven't bowed down to kiss Baal's images."

So Elijah set out from Mount Horeb. He found Elisha working in the fields at Abelmeholah. Twelve yoke of oxen pulled his plow. Elijah passed by and threw his cape over Elisha's shoulders. Elisha knew he had been made a prophet like Elijah. "Let me kiss my mother and father good-bye. Then I'll follow you!" he shouted.

"Go back then," Elijah said. "If you must do that, I've done nothing for you."

Then Elisha killed his oxen and built a fire of the yokes and plow. The people nearby ate the roasted meat of the twenty-four oxen. Elisha would never plow again. He followed Elijah down the path, wearing the great prophet's cape. Elisha became Elijah's servant.

Find It in the Bible
1 KINGS 19:15–21

MURDER FOR A VINEYARD

Next to Ahab's palace was a vineyard belonging to Naboth. "Let me buy your vineyard," said Ahab. "I want to plant vegetables there."

"This vineyard was my great-grandfather's," Naboth replied. "I won't sell."

Jezebel heard Ahab was angry. He couldn't have Naboth's vineyard. She plotted, had Naboth killed, and called Ahab. "Take Naboth's vineyard," she said. "He's dead."

Ahab and Jezebel walked in the vineyard. Elijah appeared. "God will make your family like Jeroboam's," he said. "They'll be destroyed for what you've done. As for you, Jezebel, the dogs will gnaw on your bones in Jezreel."

Find It in the Bible
1 KINGS 21:1–29

ELIJAH'S FINAL JOURNEY

Ahab died a coward in a battle with Syria. His son Ahaziah ruled in his place. After two years, he fell out of a window in his palace and died. Since Ahaziah didn't have a son, his brother, Jehoram, became king.

Meanwhile, the prophet Elijah's work in Israel was done. Elijah and Elisha were on the way from Gilgal. "The Lord has sent me to Bethel," the prophet said to Elisha. "You stay here."

"Just as sure as God is living, I won't leave you." Elisha knew Elijah would soon be taken by God.

Next they came to Jericho. Some of Elijah's followers came to Elisha. "Do you know that today God will take your master from you?" they asked.

"Yes, I know," he replied. "Keep silent."

Elijah said, "Stay here. God has sent me to the Jordan River." But Elisha refused to leave. Together they walked to the river. Fifty of the prophet's followers stood watching nearby. Elijah took off his cape, rolled it up, and hit the water with it. The river divided and the two prophets crossed on dry ground.

Find It in the Bible
2 KINGS 2:1–8

ELIJAH SOARS IN A WHIRLWIND

Tell me, Elisha. What can I do for you before I'm taken?" Elijah asked.

"Please give me a double share of your spirit," Elisha said.

"That is hard. But if you see me as I'm taken away, it's yours."

The two prophets continued walking and talking. Suddenly, a chariot of fire pulled by flaming horses divided them. Elijah soared in a whirlwind into heaven.

Elisha watched, crying out, "Father, Father! The chariots of Israel and its horsemen!" When Elijah was out of sight, Elisha tore his clothes in grief.

Find It in the Bible
2 KINGS 2:9–12

"ELISHA HAS ELIJAH'S SPIRIT"

Elijah's cape lay nearby. It had fallen from his shoulders during the whirlwind. Elisha picked it up, walked back, and stood on the riverbank. He took the cape and hit the water. "Where is the Lord, the God of Elijah?" he said. Again the river divided, and Elisha walked across on dry ground.

On the other side, the prophet's followers were waiting. "Elisha has Elijah's spirit," they declared and bowed down to Elisha. "Let us send fifty men to search for your master. Maybe he's fallen into a valley."

"No, don't send them," Elisha replied. But they urged him until he gave in and said, "Send them."

For three days they searched but didn't find Elijah. When they returned, Elisha said, "Didn't I tell you not to go?"

People from Jericho came to Elisha. "This city is beautiful," they said. "But the water is bad and the land doesn't give us fruit."

"Bring me a brand-new bottle and fill it with salt." Throwing the salt in the city's spring, Elisha spoke: "The Lord says, 'I've made this water healthy. No sickness or death will come from it again.' " Jericho has had good water ever since.

Find It in the Bible
2 KINGS 2:13–22

ELISHA'S WORKS OF POWER

Elisha traveled around Israel visiting the people. One day a woman came to him. "My husband's dead," she said. "You know that he feared the Lord. But he owed money when he died. They want to take my children as slaves in payment."

"Do you have anything to pay them?" Elisha asked.

"All I have is a jar of oil."

"Go and borrow as many empty jars as you can. Fill the jars with oil."

The neighbors brought jars, and she kept pouring oil. Every jar she could find was filled.

"Go sell the oil and pay your debts," the prophet said. "You and your children live on the rest."

Men were cutting logs by the Jordan River. While one worked, his axehead fell into the water. He cried, "Master, this is a borrowed axe!" In those days iron was hard to get. Elisha threw a stick in the water. The axehead floated to the surface like it was wood.

Such works of power showed Israel that Elisha was God's prophet.

Find It in the Bible
2 Kings 4:1–7; 6:1–7

ELISHA CURES A GREAT LEPER

The great leader of Syria's army was named Naaman. He had a terrible skin disease called leprosy. An Israelite girl was Naaman's slave. "Elisha could cure my master," she said.

Soon, Naaman traveled to Elisha's house in Samaria. He sent his servant, Gehazi, to meet Naaman. "Elisha says, 'Wash in the Jordan River seven times. Your skin will become pure.' "

"Why didn't Elisha come out?" Naaman complained. He went away in a rage.

Naaman's servants said, "Master, suppose the prophet had said to do something difficult. Wouldn't you have done it? All Elisha said was, 'Wash, and be clean. Why not do it?' "

So Naaman went to the river and bathed. His skin became like a young boy's. Then he returned to the prophet. "I know there is a God in Israel," he said. "Take this gift for what you've done." Elisha refused the gift.

As the caravan left, Gehazi followed. "Elisha needs the gift now," he lied, taking the gold. But Elisha knew, and Gehazi went away white with leprosy.

Find It in the Bible
2 Kings 5:1–27

ISRAEL'S CHARIOTS OF FIRE

Syria and Israel were at war throughout Elisha's life. Syria's king thought there was a spy in his army. But he was told, "There's no spy; it's Elisha, the prophet."

"Where is he?" the king demanded.

"He's in Dothan."

Horses, chariots, and a great army were sent to capture Elisha. At night they surrounded the city. Elisha's servant rose early. There were horses and chariots all around. "Oh no!" he cried. "Master, what shall we do?"

"Don't be afraid," assured the prophet. "There are more with us than there are with them." Then Elisha prayed: "Lord, please help my servant see." He saw the mountains full of horses and chariots of fire all around. When the Syrians came down against him, Elisha prayed: "Please strike these people blind."

Elisha led the blinded Syrian army into Israel. Israel's king asked, "Elisha, should we kill them?"

"You didn't capture them," he answered. "Why would you kill them? Serve them a feast and let them return to their king." The Syrians then stopped their attacks on Israel.

Find It in the Bible
2 KINGS 6:8–23

THE LEPERS AND THE EMPTY CAMP

Syria surrounded the city of Samaria and the people were starving. Elisha encouraged the king not to give up. "Tomorrow there will be plenty of cheap food in Samaria," he said.

A nobleman scoffed, "Only if food rains from heaven."

"You'll see it with your eyes, but you won't eat any."

That night the Lord worked. He caused the Syrians to hear the sound of a huge army. They all ran from their camp and left everthing behind. Four lepers found the camp empty and unguarded. They ran to Samaria with the good news.

Find It in the Bible
2 KINGS 6:24–7:11

THE RUSH FOR THE SYRIANS' FOOD

The king of Israel heard the news about the Syrian camp. But he thought it was a trap. "If we come out of the city they'll capture us," he thought. So he sent two men out on horseback. They followed the road all the way to the Jordan River. It was littered with clothes and weapons thrown off by the fleeing army.

When the news came to Samaria, everyone rushed to the gate. They waited there for food from the Syrian camp. When it came, there was more than enough for all the people. The food was sold cheaply just as Elisha said it would be.

The king chose the scoffing nobleman to supervise at the gate. He had laughed at Elisha: "Only if food rains from heaven."

"You'll see it with your eyes, but you won't eat any," the prophet had answered. At the gate, the nobleman saw that Elisha was right. Many people were starving. They rushed to get the food. But the nobleman ate none of it. He was knocked to the ground by the crowd and crushed to death.

Find It in the Bible
2 KINGS 7:12–20

HAZAEL SMOTHERS THE KING

Long before this, God spoke to Elijah out of the silence. That day, he told Elijah to anoint two kings: Hazael, king of Syria, and Jehu, king of Israel. This job fell to Elijah's servant, Elisha.

The day Elisha came to Syria, King Benhadad was sick. He sent Hazael to the prophet. "Ask Elisha if I'll get well." Hazael took gifts and went to the prophet.

Elisha said to Hazael, "He will get well. But the Lord has also said he will die." Elisha looked at Hazael and began to weep.

"Why do you cry, my lord?"

"Because I know the evil you will do in Israel. You will kill men, women, and children."

"I'm no better than a dog. How could I do these things?"

Elisha answered, "The Lord has said you'll be Syria's king."

Hazael returned to King Benhadad. "The man of God said that you'll get well." The next day Hazael came in while the king was asleep. He took the bedspread and dipped it in water. Then Hazael pressed it on Benhadad's face and smothered him. Hazael became king over Syria.

Find It in the Bible
2 Kings 8:7–15

DAY 149
A CAPTAIN BECOMES KING

"Take this oil," Elisha said to a young prophet. "Go to Ramoth-gilead. Find Jehu. Then say, 'The Lord says this: I've anointed you king over Israel.' When you're done, come back right away."

The young prophet took the flask of oil to Ramoth-gilead. He found the captains sitting together in Israel's camp. "I have a message for you, Commander," he said.

"For which one of us?" Jehu asked.

"The message is for you, sir."

The prophet poured the oil on Jehu's head. "The Lord says this: 'I've anointed you as king over my people Israel.' You'll destroy Ahab's family because they killed God's prophets." Then the prophet left.

"Why did that madman come to you?" the others asked Jehu.

"No reason. You know how they babble."

"Tell us the truth."

"I've just been anointed king over Israel."

The captains threw their robes in front of Jehu's feet. A trumpet blared, and they all shouted, "Jehu is king!"

Find It in the Bible
2 KINGS 9:1–15

TREASON, TREACHERY, AND WITCHCRAFT

The watchman at Jezreel looked across the countryside. "I see a company of soldiers," he reported. "Jehu must be leading them. He drives like a maniac. Maybe he has news of the battle with Syria."

Judah's King Ahaziah was in Jezreel visiting King Joram of Israel. They set out in their chariots, hoping for news. Jehu had other plans because of the young prophet's words: "Destroy Ahab's family."

"Is it peace?" Joram asked.

"How can there be peace?" Jehu answered. "Never while your mother Jezebel still practices witchcraft."

Joram turned his horses and ran, shouting, "Treason, Ahaziah!"

Find It in the Bible
2 KINGS 9:16–23

JEHU DESTROYS AHAB'S FAMILY

Treason, Ahaziah!" Joram wheeled his chariot and ran. Jehu drew his bow with all his strength. The arrow pierced Joram's heart. King Ahaziah drove his horses the other way. Jehu and his men took chase.

"Shoot him also." And they did. Ahaziah drove as far as Megiddo and died there. His officers took him to Jerusalem where he was buried.

Jezebel heard the news: "Jehu is in Jezreel." She put on her makeup and her crown. Jezebel saw Jehu enter the gates.

She called to him: "Is it peace, Jehu?"

"Throw her out the window!" he shouted. Jezebel fell to the ground and was trampled by horses. Later, Jehu ordered that Jezebel be buried. But her body was gone, eaten by dogs, as Elijah said.

Elijah also had said that Ahab's family would be completely destroyed. Jehu did this, killing Ahab's seventy sons. He destroyed Baal's priests in their own temple. Baal was never worshiped again in Israel.

God was pleased with Jehu's work. "Your sons will rule Israel," he said. "Your great-grandson will sit on the throne."

Find It in the Bible
2 KINGS 9:23–10:30

ELISHA'S LIFE-GIVING BONES

Joash, Jehu's grandson, was Israel's king when Elisha was about to die. "My father, my father!" Joash wept. "You're more important than Israel's horses and chariots."

"Take a bow and arrows and draw back the bowstring," said Elisha.

Elisha put his hands on the king's hands. "Open the window and shoot." And Joash did so. "This is the Lord's arrow of victory over Syria."

"Now take the arrows and hit the ground with them." Joash hit the ground with the arrows three times. "Why did you stop? You should have hit the ground five or six times. Then you would have had that many victories. Now you'll beat Syria three times and no more."

Soon Elisha died and was buried in a cave. The next year a band of Moabites buried a man in the same place. When this man's body touched Elisha's bones, life returned to it and the Moabite stood up on his feet.

True to Elisha's word, Israel defeated Syria three times. Israel's captured cities were taken back from Syria's control.

Find It in the Bible
2 Kings 13:14–25

JONAH RUNS FROM THE CREATOR

Syria was losing power. But Assyria was rising up. Its capital city, Nineveh, was huge. A man would take three days to walk through it. Israel was in danger of falling under Assyria's power. At that time, the Lord spoke to Jonah. "Go to Nineveh. Cry out and speak to them. I know of their wickedness."

Jonah didn't want to do this. Instead, he went the other way, to the seaport at Joppa. There he sailed for Tarshish, still further from Nineveh. But the Lord threw a great wind onto the sea. There was a mighty storm. The ship was in danger and her crew each prayed to his god.

They lightened the ship's load by throwing cargo overboard. That's when they discovered Jonah sleeping in the hold. "How can you sleep at a time like this? Get up. Call on your God to save us."

"We must find the man who has caused our distress." So the sailors decided to draw straws. Jonah lost the draw.

"I'm running away from the God who created the sea and land," he told them. Then the sailors were even more afraid.

"No wonder this has happened." They trembled.

Find It in the Bible
JONAH 1:1–11

DAY 154
A FISH SPITS OUT JONAH

The waves were running high. The ship was in danger. "What shall we do to calm the sea?" the sailors asked.

"Throw me into the sea," Jonah answered. "I've caused this trouble." But the sailors tried to row to shore. Finally, they could do no more. Praying for forgiveness, they threw Jonah overboard. Immediately, the sea stopped raging.

The Lord sent a big fish to swallow Jonah. He was in its belly for three days and nights. Jonah prayed to God from within the fish. The Lord spoke to the fish. It spit Jonah onto the beach.

Find It in the Bible
JONAH 1:11–2:10

A LITTLE PLANT AND A GREAT CITY

Jonah, get up and go to Nineveh," God said. "Speak the message I give you." This time, Jonah went. He walked all day into the city. There he cried out, "In forty days, Nineveh will be torn down."

The people of Nineveh believed God and turned from their sins. Nineveh's king declared, "No one may eat or drink. All must pray to God. Who knows? God may change his mind so we don't die." When God saw this, he did change his mind. He didn't slaughter Nineveh.

Jonah was angry. "This is why I ran away in the first place," he prayed. "I knew you were a God of love. You're always ready to change your mind about punishing people. Take my life; it's better that I die."

East of the city, Jonah built a hut. There he sat watching. What would happen to Nineveh? God made a plant grow there to give cool shade. This made Jonah happy. Then the plant died, and Jonah suffered in the heat. He was sorry the plant died.

"You were sorry a little plant died," God said. "What about this great city? Shouldn't I have pity on its little children?"

Find It in the Bible
JONAH 3:1–4:11

ISRAEL CARRIED TO CAPTIVITY

Israel became weak and helpless. Her kings were murderers and idol worshipers. The Assyrians won many victories in war. Israelites were captured and carried away. Those left were robbed of all they had.

Nineteen kings ruled the ten tribes who lived in Israel. The first was Jeroboam; the last was Hoshea. In Hoshea's time, Shalmanezer, king of Assyria, came to Samaria with a great army. He surrounded the city. No one could go in or come out. But Samaria was built on a hill. Shalmanezer couldn't take the city easily and died before the victory. Sargon became king in his place.

In three years, Samaria fell to Assyria. Sargon killed Hoshea. Nearly all the people were carried away from the land. They went to faraway countries in the east: Mesopotamia, Media, and lands near the Caspian Sea.

In these distant lands, the people of Israel changed forever. They married the foreign people and worshiped their gods. They lost all knowledge of the Lord who rescued them from Egypt. This was the end of the ten tribes. They never saw their own land again. God's ancient tribes became lost among the peoples of the Far East.

Find It in the Bible
2 KINGS 17:1–41

THE LAW IS TAUGHT IN JUDAH

South of Israel was the kingdom of Judah. Its main city was Jerusalem. There stood Solomon's temple and the king's palace. Rehoboam was Solomon's son. He and his son after him left the Lord, and Judah suffered. Then Asa, Rehoboam's grandson, became king. He rebuilt the altar that had rotted away and began proper worship. He burned all the idols in the land. But when he died, idol worship returned.

Jehoshaphat was Asa's son. His heart was brave in the Lord's ways. He, too, destroyed the idols. He sent men throughout the land teaching the Lord's law.

Find It in the Bible
2 CHRONICLES 12:1–17:9

JEHORAM'S AWFUL DEATH

Jehoshaphat was a good and wise king in Judah. But he made one big mistake: He allowed his son Jehoram to marry Athaliah. She was the daughter of Ahab and Jezebel.

Elijah was living in Israel when Jehoram was king of Judah. A letter came to King Jehoram from the prophet. Elijah wrote: "God says, 'You aren't living like your father Jehoshaphat or grandfather Asa did. Instead, you live like Ahab and the kings of Israel. You've led Judah to turn away from me. Ahab did the same thing in Israel. Not only so, you killed your own brothers, and they were better than you. So God will bring a disease on you and your family. All your insides are going to come out because of the disease.' "

The Lord sent the Philistines and Arabians against Judah. They took away everything of the king's. They captured his wives and all his children but the youngest. Then the Lord gave him a disease in his stomach. It couldn't be cured. In two years, Jehoram's insides fell out. He died in agony. No one was sorry. Jehoram wasn't even buried with Judah's kings.

Find It in the Bible
2 CHRONICLES 21:1–20

THE HIDDEN BOY BECOMES KING

After Jehoram died, his son, Ahaziah, became king in Judah. One year after Ahaziah became king, he was with King Joram in Israel. Jehu killed Ahaziah when he killed Joram and Ahab's family. That day, Athaliah's son Ahaziah, brother Joram, and mother Jezebel all died. Athaliah was enraged and killed all the royal family of Judah.

Only Ahaziah's youngest son survived—the baby Joash. Ahaziah's sister, Jehoshabeath, hid Joash in the temple.

Meanwhile Athaliah made herself queen in Judah. She stopped the Lord's worship, built a temple for Baal, and led the idol worship.

Seven years later, Joash was ready. Jehoiada brought young Joash out of the temple to the people. Jehoiada put the crown on him and the people shouted, "Long live the king!"

The sound of praise brought Queen Athaliah from her palace. "Treason, treason!" she cried as she ran into the temple.

"Take this woman out of the Lord's house," commanded Jehoida. Athaliah was dragged out and killed. And so David's royal family ruled again in Judah.

Find It in the Bible
2 CHRONICLES 22:1–23:21

DAY 160
JOASH REPAIRS THE TEMPLE

Joash was seven years old when he began to reign. As a man, Joash decided to repair Solomon's temple. It was very old and had been mistreated over the years.

Outside the temple doors, Joash placed a large box. He announced that everyone should bring their gifts to the temple. The people were glad to do this. Day after day, the box was filled with money.

Joash and Jehoiada the priest gave the money to hire workmen. Carpenters, metalworkers, laborers, and craftsmen worked. They repaired the Lord's house. Judah worshiped there until Jehoiada died.

Find It in the Bible
2 CHRONICLES 24:1–15

ISRAEL ROBS THE TEMPLE

Judah's princes loved to worship idols. The good priest Jehoiada was dead. So the king listened to the princes. They talked him into leaving the Lord. So again, the Lord allowed the Syrians to attack. They beat Judah's larger army and wounded Joash. Later, the king's own servants killed him. Joash ruled Judah forty years. But he wasn't buried with Judah's kings.

Amaziah, Joash's son, began to rule at age twenty-five. He raised an army of 300,000 to attack Edom. He paid Israel 7,500 pounds of silver for an army of 100,000 to help. But a prophet told him, "Don't let Israel's army go with you. God isn't with them."

"But how will I get back my silver?"

"God can give you much more than you lost."

Amaziah won the battle without Israel's army. But he brought back Edom's idols to Jerusalem. A prophet asked him, "These gods couldn't save Edom from your army. Why do you turn to them?" Amaziah wouldn't listen.

So Israel's army attacked Judah. They broke down Jerusalem's wall, robbed the temple, and kidnapped the king. Fifteen years later, Amaziah died and was buried with Judah's kings.

Find It in the Bible
2 CHRONICLES 24:17–25:28

THE PRIDE OF UZZIAH

Amaziah's sixteen-year-old son, Uzziah, became king. Living in the Lord's way, he strengthened the kingdom. Uzziah was victorious in war and built fortified cities in Judah. He loved the fields, so trees, vineyards, and crops flourished.

But when Uzziah became strong, he became proud. He was already king, but he wanted to be the priest, too. One day, he went into the temple to offer incense. Eighty-one priests followed.

"Leave here," they warned. "This is trouble for you."

Holding the incense, Uzziah got angry. Just then, leprosy broke out on his forehead.

Find It in the Bible
2 CHRONICLES 26:1–20

DAY 163
GOD CALLS ISAIAH

Ahaz was the son of a good king, Jotham, who believed in God. But he worshiped Baal and burned his sons as sacrifices. Ahaz made sacrifices—on hills, in valleys, and under every green tree.

When Edom attacked Judah, Ahaz asked Assyria for help. But instead of helping, they took over Judah. Ahaz was robbed of everything because of his sins. Judah was oppressed under Assyria.

God's prophet Isaiah lived in the days of these kings. Isaiah was worshiping in the temple when he saw God on his throne surrounded by angels. The temple shook with voices: "Holy, holy is the Lord of hosts."

Isaiah trembled, saying, "I'm a man with unclean lips, yet I've seen the Lord God." Then an angel brought a coal from the altar. The burning coal touched Isaiah's lips.

"Your sin is taken away. You are made clean."

The Lord said, "Who will be my messenger to the people?"

"Here I am, Lord," Isaiah said. "Send me."

The Lord replied, "Go and speak to my people."

Find It in the Bible
2 Chronicles 28:1–27; Isaiah 6:1–9

A TREE WILL GROW FROM A STUMP

The Lord called Isaiah and said, "You'll be my prophet. Go to the people and speak my words. They'll listen but won't catch my meaning. They'll see but won't understand. Your words will do them no good. Instead, you'll make their minds dull. Close their ears, and shut their eyes. Then they won't use their eyes to look. They won't use their ears to hear. They won't understand with their minds, turn to me, and be healed."

Isaiah asked, "How long will this be, Lord?"

"Until the cities become wastelands where no one lives. Until the houses are empty and the land is barren. This must be until I send everyone to a faraway place; until the land is totally empty. My people will be like an oak tree—cut to the ground. The stump is all that's left behind. Out of its roots a new tree will grow."

Isaiah's words seemed to do no good when he spoke them. But the Lord wanted him to continue speaking to his people. Sometime, far in the future, Judah would be restored to serve God.

Find It in the Bible
ISAIAH 6:9–13

HEZEKIAH CLEANS THE TEMPLE

Hezekiah, Ahaz's son, reigned next. The first thing he did was repair the temple doors. With its doors opened, he ordered the temple cleaned.

"Our ancestors have been untrue to God," Hezekiah told the priests. "They've done evil and turned from the Lord. The Lord's house has been forgotten. They put out its lamps, closed its doors, and walked away. Our ancestors stopped offering incense and burning sacrifices to Israel's God. This is why God's anger came upon Judah and Jerusalem. Their lives filled with horror. It was an amazing mockery, as you've seen."

Hezekiah went on speaking to the priests. "Our fathers have been killed by the sword. Our sons, daughters, and wives have been carried far away. In my heart, I want to make an agreement with God. I want to turn his fierce anger away from us. So don't be lazy. God has chosen you to minister to him and give him offerings."

The priests went into the deepest part of the temple. There they found hateful idols. These were burned at Jerusalem's dump. They worked for over two weeks and purified the Lord's house.

Find It in the Bible
2 CHRONICLES 29:1–19

HEZEKIAH'S VICTORY OVER ASSYRIA

Hezekiah followed God with his whole heart. King Sennacherib's Assyrian army invaded Judah, but Hezekiah shut off Judah's water supply. "Why should Assyria find water?" he reasoned.

They strengthened Jerusalem's wall. Many new weapons were made for the fight. Then Hezekiah called the people together. "Be strong," he said. "Don't be afraid of Sennacherib or his horde. There is one with us who is greater than those with him. Sennacherib has only human strength. But the Lord is here to help us and fight our battles."

Messengers came from Assyria. They shouted to the people inside Jerusalem. They said terrible things about God, trying to shake their faith. Because of this, Hezekiah and Isaiah prayed. The Lord sent an angel into the Assyrian camp. This angel killed the leading warriors there. Sennacherib had to return to Assyria in disgrace. There his sons murdered him.

So the Lord saved Jerusalem from her enemies and gave them rest. Hezekiah became famous in all the nations.

Find It in the Bible
2 CHRONICLES 32:1–23

THE SUNDIAL MOVES BACKWARDS

The Assyrians had invaded Judah. Jerusalem was in danger. King Hezekiah became sick and was near death. Isaiah the prophet came to speak with him.

"The Lord says: 'Get your life prepared, because you will die. You'll not get better.'"

Hezekiah prayed: "Remember, O Lord, how I've been faithful to you. I've done what is good for you with my whole heart."

Isaiah was walking away from the palace. "Turn," God said, "and talk with Hezekiah again. Say, 'The God of your ancestor David says: I've heard your prayer and seen your tears. I'll heal you and add fifteen years to your life. The city will be saved from Assyria.'"

"How will the Lord prove that he will heal me?" Hezekiah asked Isaiah.

"You choose the sign," answered Isaiah. "Shall the sundial gain ten minutes or lose ten minutes?"

"It normally gains time. Let the shadow go backwards."

Isaiah cried to God and the shadow moved backwards by ten minutes. In three days, Hezekiah was well.

Find It in the Bible
2 KINGS 20:1–21

DAY 168
MANASSEH'S REPENTANCE

T he son of Hezekiah was twelve years old when he became king. His name was Manasseh. He did evil things. He rebuilt the idols' altars and worshiped Baal, even putting idols in the temple. Manasseh burned his own sons as offerings and practiced witchcraft. The people followed Manasseh into evil. They became more disgusting than the tribes Israel had driven out of Canaan. God was pushed to great anger.

"Manasseh has been horrible," God declared. "I'm going to bring much evil on Jerusalem. When people hear of it, their ears will tingle. I'll turn it over and discard my people. They've been causing me anger since the day they left Egypt." Manasseh ignored God's words.

Manasseh was captured by Assyria's army. He was carried in chains to Babylon. There he was tormented. So he turned back to God. The Lord heard his prayer and returned him to Jerusalem as king. Then Manasseh knew that the Lord was God.

Safe in Jerusalem, Manasseh destroyed the idols. He began the true worship of God and commanded Judah to serve the Lord. Manasseh died after fifty-five years as king.

Find It in the Bible
2 KINGS 21:1–20

JOSIAH CLEARS IDOLS FROM THE LAND

Amon, Manasseh's son, reigned two years. He was killed by his own servants and his son Josiah reigned. Josiah was eight years old when his father died. When Josiah was sixteen years old, he began to seek God. When he was twenty, he cleared the land of idols. No king before had so completely destroyed idols in Judah. He even went outside Judah breaking altars and burning images. Josiah dug up the bones of the idols' priests. He burned the priests' bones with the idols they worshiped.

Two hundred years before, Jeroboam had set up a golden calf in Bethel north of Jerusalem. Josiah burned that idol and crushed it to dust. The bones of the idol priests were burned on their altars. There Josiah found a grave. "What is that grave marker I see?" he asked.

"This is the grave of the man of God from Judah. He came here when Jeroboam was offering incense. This prophet predicted that you would do what you're doing today."

"Let him rest," Josiah said. "No one should move his bones."

Find It in the Bible
2 Kings 21:19–23:20

GOD'S LOST LAW IS FOUND

While Josiah was destroying idols, others were repairing the temple. There they found an old book written on rolls of leather. This was the book of the law that God gave to Moses. It had been hidden so long that it was forgotten. Saphan brought the book to King Josiah.

Josiah heard the law read for the first time in many years. Terrified, he directed, "Go and seek the Lord. Someone must know about the law. We've had all these troubles because our ancestors ignored God's word."

Huldah the prophetess lived in Jerusalem. She could understand God's law.

Find It in the Bible
2 CHRONICLES 34:8–22

THE DEATH OF JOSIAH

The Lord speaks," said Huldah the prophetess. " 'Tell the man who sent you that I'll bring disaster. This place will know all the curses written in the law. Judah has left me and made offerings to other gods. This has pushed me to anger. My endless rage will pour out on this place. But the king of Judah's heart was good toward me. He'll die in peace. Josiah won't see the disaster I'll bring here.' "

King Josiah called the priests, princes, and people to the temple. He read to them the book of the law. Then they all promised to serve the Lord and keep his law. They kept this promise while Josiah lived.

The kingdom of Judah was a part of the great empire of Assyria. But Assyria was getting weak. Pharaoh Necho of Egypt passed through Judah to attack Assyria. "I've nothing against you," he told Josiah. "So don't stand in my way, or you'll be destroyed."

But Josiah and his army met Egypt in battle. The king was killed in his chariot, brought to Jerusalem, and buried. The prophet Jeremiah and all the people mourned for the last hope of Judah.

Find It in the Bible
2 CHRONICLES 34:22–35:27

JEHOIAKIM BURNS GOD'S WORDS

Josiah was killed in battle and buried in honor. The people made his son, Jehoahaz, the new king. But Pharaoh Necho, the new emperor over Judah, didn't trust Jehoahaz. Judah's king was taken captive to Egypt.

Jeremiah said, "Don't weep for the dead Josiah. Weep instead for the one who goes away, King Jehoahaz. He'll never come back or see his land again. He'll die in his prison."

Pharaoh made Jehoahaz's brother, Jehoiakim, king of Judah. He led the people back to idol worship. Jeremiah warned him against this and Jehoiakim was angry. He tried to kill the prophet. But Jeremiah was hidden by his friends; later, Jeremiah's friend Barach read his prophecy to the people.

Soldiers took Jeremiah's scroll to King Jehoiakim. As it was read to him, the king burned the scroll. His own princes begged the king not to do this. They knew Jeremiah spoke God's word for Judah. But Jehoiakim ignored them.

Soon Babylon defeated Egypt. Nebuchadnezzar of Babylon attacked Jerusalem and Jehoiakim surrendered. But soon he was killed, and his body was thrown out of Jerusalem.

Find It in the Bible
2 KINGS 23:31–24:1; 2 CHRONICLES 36:1–7

JEREMIAH'S VISION OF THE FIGS

Jehoiakim's young son, Jehoiachin, was made Judah's king. But Nebuchadnezzar, Babylon's king, overran Jerusalem and Judah. He captured the king and other nobles and took them to Babylon.

After this Jeremiah had a vision of the future. He saw two baskets of figs. "What do you see, Jeremiah?" the Lord asked.

"Figs. The good figs are very good. The bad ones are so bad they can't be eaten."

The Lord explained this. "The captives taken to Babylon are like the good figs. I'll care for them and bring them back to this land. They'll be my people and I'll be their God. The bad figs are like the people left in the land. These include their king, Zedekiah, his princes, and his people. They will suffer and be killed. Plagues and famine will come to them until they are no more."

So Jeremiah wrote to the captives in Babylon. "Build houses, plant gardens, and have children. Let them be married in that land when they grow. After seventy years, you'll return to your own land in peace. God's thoughts are of peace and kindness toward you."

Find It in the Bible
JEREMIAH 24:1–10

DAY 174
JEREMIAH IN A MUDDY PIT

Nebuchadnezzar carried the captives away and made Zedekiah king. Zedekiah promised to serve Nebuchadnezzar. Soon the promise was broken. He also began to pray to false gods who couldn't help him.

Jeremiah warned Zedekiah: "You're going to be handed over to the king of Babylon. The people who go with the Babylonians will live. Those who stay to fight will die in battle and famine."

Angered, Zedekiah threw Jeremiah in a muddy prison pit. He was left to die. But an Ethiopian named Ebedimelech asked permission and rescued Jeremiah. Ebedimelech pulled him up from the pit with ropes.

Find It in the Bible
JEREMIAH 37:1–38:13

DAY 175
THE DESTRUCTION OF JERUSALEM

Nebuchadnezzar surrounded Jerusalem. The people were trapped, starving, and sick. Finally, the soldiers of Babylon broke through the wall. All of the treasures in the temple and the palaces were carried away.

Soldiers burned the temple and all of the houses, and ruined the wall of Jerusalem. The people who remained were made Nebuchadnezzar's servants. The Babylonian king slaughtered Zedekiah's sons before his eyes. He killed Judah's princes and gouged out Zedekiah's eyes. Judah's last king was dragged off in chains to Babylon.

Jeremiah was freed and given the choice: Go to Babylon or stay in the land. Jeremiah chose to stay in the land God had promised to Abraham. But when the remnant of people chose to go to Egypt, Jeremiah went with them. Jeremiah is called the weeping prophet because he wept for the peoples' sins.

King Nebuchadnezzar returned to Babylon with the treasures of Jerusalem. God's people were his captives. Four hundred years had passed since Judah's first king, Rehoboam. The city of David was blackened rubble. Solomon's temple was a heap of ashes.

Find It in the Bible
JEREMIAH 39:1–10; 2 CHRONICLES 36:15–21

THE SONGS OF ZION

The captives in Babylon didn't forget their beloved homeland. Their children learned songs which taught them their history. Though they were often sad, they could still sing such songs:

> By the rivers of Babylon—there we sat
>   down and there we wept when we
>   remembered Zion.
> On the willows there we hung up our harps.
> For there our captors asked us for songs,
>   and our tormentors asked for mirth,
>   saying, "Sing us one of the songs of
>   Zion."
>
> How could we sing the Lord's song
>   in a foreign land?
> If I forget you, O Jerusalem,
>   let my right hand wither!
> Let my tongue cling to the roof of my mouth,
>   if I do not remember you,
>   if I do not set Jerusalem
>   above my highest joy.

Find It in the Bible
PSALM 137:1–6

DAY 177
THE VALLEY OF DRY BONES

The Lord sent prophets to the Israelites even in Babylon. Ezekiel prophesied about Israel's future:

"The Lord's spirit brought me to a valley. It was full of bones. There were many, many bones all around, and they were very dry. The Lord asked me, 'Man, can these bones live?'

"'You know, Lord,' I answered.

"'Then speak to them. Tell them the Lord says this: I'll make breath come into you and you'll live. I'll make muscles and skin to come onto you. I'll give you breath. Then you'll know that I'm the Lord.'

"So I spoke these things to the dry bones. Suddenly, there was a noise. I heard rattling, and the bones came together. Muscles and skin covered them. I spoke to the four winds and breath entered the bodies. They were alive, standing on their feet.

"'This is the nation of Israel. Tell them that I'll bring you up from captivity. I'll bring you back to the land of Israel. I'll put my spirit in you and you'll live. Then you'll know that your God has spoken and will act.'"

Find It in the Bible
EZEKIEL 37:1–28

DAY 178
DANIEL AND HIS FRIENDS

Among the captives in Babylon was a young man named Daniel. God prepared him to become a great prophet of Israel.

King Nebuchadnezzar wanted young Jews to serve in his palace. They were to be bright, handsome, strong young men. Each must learn the Babylonian language and read its books. Wise men would teach them for three years. Then they would have jobs in the royal palace.

Among them were Daniel, Hananiah, Mishael, and Azariah. These men were from Judah. The king ordered they be given Babylonian names. They were then called Belteshazzar, Shadrach, Meshach, and Abednego.

Find It in the Bible
DANIEL 1:1-7

THE VIRTUE OF DANIEL

Daniel and his friends came to Nebuchadnezzar's palace. But their food had been offered to idols. Daniel went to the palace master. "Please don't make me dishonor myself by eating food given to idols."

"The king himself has given you this food. If you don't eat it, you won't be healthy. Then my life could be in danger of the king's anger."

"Let's try it for ten days," Daniel suggested. "Just give us vegetables to eat and water to drink. Then see if we're healthy."

The palace master agreed. After ten days, Daniel and his three friends looked healthier than the others. So they never ate the idols' food. God gave these four wisdom and skill in Babylonian knowledge. Daniel also could understand dreams and visions.

After three years' training they were brought to Nebuchadnezzar. The king spoke with them. No one could compare with Daniel, Hananiah, Mishael, and Azariah. They became part of the king's own court. The king was pleased. These four were ten times better than his own magicians and psychics.

Find It in the Bible
DANIEL 1:8–21

DANIEL'S GOOD JUDGMENT

King Nebuchadnezzar dreamed a troubling dream. So he called his magicians and psychics. "I must know the meaning of my dream."

"Tell us the dream, O king. We'll show you its meaning."

"No. You must tell me both the dream and its meaning. If you don't, I'll have you killed; if you do, you'll be wealthy."

Fearful, the magicians and psychics said, "No one on earth can do what you ask. Only our gods could tell you your own dream."

The king flew into a violent rage. "Destroy all the wise men in Babylon," he commanded. This order included Daniel and his friends.

Daniel used good judgment talking with the king's executioner. He was able to gain time from the king. The four friends prayed to God about the dream. They asked that they and the Babylonian wise men wouldn't die. That night the Lord gave Daniel the secret of the dream.

"Don't kill the wise men," he told the executioner. "I'll show the king his dream and its meaning."

Find It in the Bible
DANIEL 2:1–24

KING NEBUCHADNEZZAR'S DREAM

No psychic can tell the mystery of your dream." Daniel spoke to King Nebuchadnezzar. "But there's a God in heaven who opens mysteries. You saw a huge, shining statue. Its head was made of gold. Its chest and arms were silver. Its middle and thighs were bronze. Its legs, iron. Its feet, part iron, part clay.

"As you watched, a stone was cut out, not by human hands. This stone hit the statue's feet of iron and clay. They broke into pieces. Then the entire statue broke into tiny pieces and blew away. The stone became a great mountain, filling the earth.

"Here is the dream's meaning: Your kingdom is the gold head. Later, another kingdom will come—the statue's silver shoulders and arms. Then a third kingdom of bronze will come. After that, a kingdom strong as iron will rise. Finally a divided kingdom that is partly strong will rule. In those days God will set up his eternal kingdom. It will end all the earth's kingdoms and grow to fill the whole earth."

Nebuchadnezzar cried in awe, "Your God is the God of gods!"

Find It in the Bible
DANIEL 2:17–49

THE FURNACE OF BLAZING FIRE

Nebuchadnezzar made a golden statue ninety feet tall. An announcement was made to everyone to worship the statue or be thrown into the furnace.

Everyone worshiped the idol Nebuchadnezzar had set up. Everyone except Shadrach, Meshach, and Abednego, the friends of Daniel. They stood before the angry king.

"You must worship the golden statue I set up. If not, you'll be thrown into the furnace."

"O Nebuchadnezzar, we can only say this: We believe our God can save us from the furnace. If he doesn't, we still won't serve your gods. Nor will we worship your golden statue."

Nebuchadnezzar was so filled with rage that his face became hideous. "Heat the furnace seven times hotter than ever before," he commanded. His strongest guards tied up Shadrach, Meshach, and Abednego.

The furnace raged with heat and killed the guards. Shadrach, Meshach, and Abednego fell down into its flames.

Find It in the Bible
DANIEL 3:1–23

FOUR MEN WALK IN THE FIRE

Nebuchadnezzar was amazed looking into the furnace. "Didn't we tie three men and throw them into the furnace?"

"This is true, O king."

"But I see four men, untied, walking through the fire. They aren't hurt at all. One of them looks like a god." Then the king called: "Shadrach, Meshach, Abednego, servants of the most high God, come out!"

The three men came out to the king. They weren't burned, nor did they smell of fire.

"The God of Shadrach, Meshach, and Abednego is blessed!" the king declared. "No one may ever speak against their God."

Find It in the Bible
DANIEL 3:24–30

GOD'S LESSON TO NEBUCHADNEZZAR
PART ONE

I, Nebuchadnezzar was living at peace. One night I had a frightening dream. So I called the wise men of Babylon to my palace. They were to tell me the meaning of my dream. But they had no idea what it meant.

"At last Daniel came to me. He's the man who's been given the spirit of the holy gods. This is the dream I told to Daniel:

"There was a very tall tree on the earth. It grew strong and its top reached to heaven. Everyone on earth could see its beautiful leaves and fruit. This tree gave food to all the people. Animals rested in its shade and birds nested in its branches. As I looked on, a holy one from heaven came. This is what he cried aloud:

" 'Cut down the tree and chop off its branches. Strip off its leaves and scatter its fruit. Let the animals run and fly away from it. Leave the tree's stump and its roots in the ground. Give him the mind of an animal and let seven years pass. Then everyone will know that God rules over the earth.'

"Now, Daniel, tell me what this means."

Find It in the Bible
DANIEL 4:1–18

GOD'S LESSON TO NEBUCHADNEZZAR

PART TWO

I hope this dream is for your enemies," Daniel said. "The tall, beautiful tree you saw, the tree that fed the whole earth, that tree is you, O king! You've grown great and strong. Your greatness reaches to heaven and your power covers the earth.

"The words of the holy one from heaven are God's command. You'll be driven away from everyone and live with wild animals. Seven years will pass. The stump means that your kingdom will return. This will happen when you learn that God is king. Take my advice. Leave your sins; care for others. Then God will give you more days of peace."

All this happened to Nebuchadnezzar. One day, he boasted of his power; the next day it was gone.

Nebuchadnezzar was driven away from everyone. He ate grass like an ox. His body was bathed in dew. His hair grew long like eagle's feathers. His fingernails were like bird's claws. After seven years, Nebuchadnezzar celebrated and honored God: "All his works are truth; his ways are just. He is able to bring low those who walk in pride."

Find It in the Bible
DANIEL 4:19–37

THE HANDWRITING ON THE WALL
PART ONE

King Cyrus and his Persian army had surrounded Babylon. But Belshazzar, the Babylonian king, was holding a great feast in honor of his god. "Bring the gold and silver cups from Solomon's temple," Belshazzar commanded. The Babylonians praised their false gods. Meanwhile, they drank from the holy cups stolen from Jerusalem.

Suddenly a hand and fingers appeared. They wrote on the palace wall. King Belshazzar was so frightened, his knees knocked together. "Call the magicians and psychics!" he commanded.

"Read this writing," Belshazzar commanded the psychics. "If you do, I'll make you rich and famous." But they couldn't read the words the hand had written.

Then the queen said, "There's a certain man in your kingdom. He has the spirit of the holy gods. Let Daniel be called. He'll read these words."

Find It in the Bible
DANIEL 5:1-12

THE HANDWRITING ON THE WALL
PART TWO

Daniel was now an old man. Belshazzar said to him: "Read the handwriting on the wall, and I'll give you money and power."

"Keep your rewards. However, I'll read the writing for you, O king. God gave your father Nebuchadnezzar this kingdom. But Nebuchadnezzar became proud and was sent away. When he became humble, Nebuchadnezzar returned. But you also are proud. You've even drunk idols' wine in cups from God's house. You haven't praised God who gives you this power. So God sent this hand to write on your wall.

"This is the writing: MENE means numbered; MENE again means numbered; TEKEL means weighed; UPHARSIN means divided. This is God's message: MENE, MENE—God has numbered the days of your kingdom. He has brought it to an end. TEKEL—You have been weighed on the scales. You are too light. UPHARSIN—Your kingdom is divided. It's been given to the Medes and Persians."

That night, Cyrus and the Persians overran Babylon.

Find It in the Bible
DANIEL 5:13–31

A LAW AGAINST PRAYER

The Persians set up Darius, a Mede, as king in Babylon. Daniel was made one of three presidents in the land. But the two other presidents were jealous of Daniel. They hatched a plan.

The presidents knew that Daniel prayed to God three times a day. So they went to Darius. "O king, everyone should pray to you and not to any other god. We want to make a new law: No one can pray to another god. If they do, throw them to the lions." Darius declared this the law.

Daniel continued praying to God.

Find It in the Bible
DANIEL 6:1–10

DANIEL IS THROWN TO THE LIONS

Despite the new law against prayer, Daniel prayed toward Jerusalem three times daily. His enemies sought to frame him and asked King Darius about the death sentence concerning the law.

"There's someone, O king, who doesn't obey this law. It is Daniel from Judah. Before the law, he prayed three times a day. And he still does."

The king was very upset that Daniel had been accused. He spent the whole day trying to save his wise president. That evening, the jealous presidents insisted that Daniel be punished.

So King Darius had to give the command. Daniel was brought and thrown into a den of lions. "You serve your God faithfully, Daniel," the king said. "I hope your God will save you from the lions." A stone was brought to seal the mouth of the cave. No one could let Daniel out of the lions' den.

Find It in the Bible
DANIEL 6:10–17

DANIEL IS SAVED FROM THE LIONS

After King Darius locked Daniel in the lions' den, he couldn't sleep. He was worried about Daniel. Early the next morning, the king ran to the lions' den.

He called, "Daniel, has God kept you safe from the lions?" The king thought he would hear the lions roar. But instead, he heard the voice of Daniel:

"God sent his angel who shut the lions' mouths. He knew I had done nothing wrong. The lions haven't hurt me." So the king took Daniel out of the den. He punished the men who were so jealous of Daniel.

Find It in the Bible
DANIEL 6:18–28

THE RELEASE FROM BABYLON

Cyrus, the emperor of Persia, was a friend of the Jews. Years before, the prophet Jeremiah had spoken about their captivity. He said the Jews would be captive in Babylon for seventy years.

Seventy years passed, and God stirred Cyrus's spirit. He commanded: "The Lord has given me all the kingdoms on earth. He has now told me to build his temple at Jerusalem in Judah. All of God's people have my permission to go up to Jerusalem. They may rebuild the house of the Lord—God be with them! Give the Jews silver and gold, goods and animals. Make offerings for the house of God in Jerusalem."

The leaders of Judah and Benjamin made ready. The priests and Levites prepared. King Cyrus himself gave them the vessels from the Lord's house—gold and silver cups, plates, and bowls. There were 5,400 vessels in all.

A total of 42,360 Jews returned to Jerusalem with this treasure. Also, 7,337 servants and 200 singers went along. The enormous caravan included 245 mules, 435 camels, and 6,720 donkeys.

Find It in the Bible
Ezra 1:1–2:67

THE REBUILDING BEGINS

The Jews returned to the ruined city. The priests, Levites, and some of the people lived in Jerusalem. The others lived in towns nearby.

After seven months, Jeshua and Zerubbabel, began to build the altar. Jeshua was the priest. Zerubbabel was the leader of the rebuilding work. They found the place of the first altar on Mount Moriah. Here, long before, Abraham had offered his son Isaac, King David had sacrificed to God, and Solomon built the first temple. The returned captives burned offerings here morning and night.

Soon work began on the temple. Builders cleared the rubble and laid the building's foundation. The priests were there with trumpets. The Levites had cymbals. They sang this song to the Lord: "For he is good, for his steady love lasts forever toward Israel."

All the people praised the Lord for laying the foundation. Many were old people. They'd seen the first temple at this place. These people wept when they saw the new foundation. Others shouted for joy. The sound of weeping blended with the shouting and was heard far away.

Find It in the Bible
Ezra 2:70–3:13

THE ENEMIES OF GOD'S BUILDING

To the north of Jerusalem lived the Samaritans. These people were a mixture of Israelites and Assyrians. They worshiped the Lord and also false gods.

The Samaritans came to Zerubbabel. "Let us help you build the temple. We worship your God. We've been sacrificing like you since we came from Assyria."

"You cannot build with us," he answered. "Only we will build for God. King Cyrus of Persia has commanded this."

So the Samaritans made the Jews afraid to build. They wrote letters and paid Persian princes to stop the work. Cyrus was far away at war and couldn't help. Soon after, he died.

Then Artaxerxes ruled the Persian Empire. He soon received a letter: "Your servants beyond the river greet you. We'd like you to know that the Jews have come to Jerusalem. They're rebuilding that wicked city and its walls. If the city is built, the Jews won't pay your taxes. We're true to you and don't want you put to shame. History shows that Jerusalem was destroyed because of its rebels. If it's rebuilt, you'll lose your power this side of the river."

Find It in the Bible
Ezra 4:1–16

THE PROPHETS OF GOD'S BUILDING

To the Samaritan leaders beyond the river," Artaxerxes replied to the enemies of God's building, "your letter has been read to me. I find that Jerusalem has had mighty kings. They ruled the whole country beyond the river. Jerusalem also warred against the kings of past empires. These people must stop their work at Jerusalem. The city cannot be rebuilt until I decide it can."

The Samaritans forced the rebuilding to stop.

Soon a new king named Darius came to power in Persia. At about that time, two prophets began speaking in Jerusalem. "Your houses are finished and God's house is in ruins," the prophet Haggai scolded the Jews. "Go to the mountains, bring wood, and build the house. Its glory will be greater than the glory of Solomon's temple.

"God's house isn't built by power." Zechariah was the other prophet who spoke for God. "Not by power, not by might, but by my spirit, says the Lord. Zerubbabel laid the temple's foundation. His hands will finish it. He'll set the top stone with shouts of 'Grace unto it!' "

So the Jews continued the building of God's house.

Find It in the Bible
EZRA 4:17–5:2

THE KING COMMANDS GOD'S BUILDING

The Jerusalem leaders wrote to King Darius. "We are rebuilding God's temple built many years ago. Our ancestors angered God. So Nebuchadnezzar destroyed this temple and carried the people away to Babylon. All of its holy vessels were placed in the temple there.

"Please search your records. Read the command of King Cyrus for the rebuilding of this temple. Then write to us your decision."

Darius searched and found a scroll. It told of Cyrus's command to rebuild the temple.

"Let the work on this house of God continue." Darius sent his command to the Samaritans. "Let the Jews rebuild this temple in its place. In fact, the cost is to be paid by your taxes. Give the Jewish priests everything they need for their sacrifices to God. And if anyone changes this command, kill him."

Find It in the Bible
EZRA 5:11–6:12

THE JEWS COMPLETE GOD'S BUILDING

The Jews rebuilt God's temple at Jerusalem helped by Haggai's and Zechariah's prophecies. They finished their building because of the command of the God of Israel. The temple was built by order of three mighty kings—Cyrus, Darius, and Artaxerxes of Persia.

The people of Israel, the priests, and the Levites celebrated. They were full of joy when the temple was dedicated. Here is the list of their offerings to God that day: one hundred bulls, two hundred rams, and four hundred lambs; as a sin offering—twelve male goats, one for each of the tribes of Israel.

Hundreds of years before, Israel had kept the first Passover in Egypt. They celebrated the Passover again in the land of God's promise. The priests were purified and the Passover lamb was killed. It was eaten by the people of Israel who had returned from Babylon. They celebrated with the Lord's joy for seven days.

The second temple was similar to Solomon's temple. There the people worshiped as before. But the ark of the covenant was lost and never returned to Jerusalem.

Find It in the Bible
EZRA 6:13–22

AN EMPIRE WITH NO QUEEN

King Darius of Persia died. His son, Ahasuerus, took his place as king. Ahasuerus gave a grand feast at his palace in Shushan. The nobles of the empire partied for 180 days. All the people in Shushan came for the final seven days. The king commanded the queen's servants to bring her into the party. He wanted everyone to see her beauty. But Queen Vashti, being modest, refused.

The king burned with anger. Vashti hadn't obeyed his command! So he had a foolish thought: "All the women in my empire will now disrespect their husbands." And Ahasuerus's kingdom was vast—it stretched from India to Ethiopia.

"What shall I do with Vashti?" the king asked his counselors.

"Never see her again. Choose another queen."

Ahasuerus sent letters throughout the empire. He declared that Vashti was no longer queen. Later, his anger cooled. Ahasuerus missed Queen Vashti. His counselors suggested, "Bring women from all the empire. Choose a new queen from among them."

So young women were brought from everywhere. Hegai, the palace servant, cared for them all.

Find It in the Bible
ESTHER 1:1–2:4

ESTHER—QUEEN OF PERSIA

Many thousands of Jews lived in the Persian Empire. Not all had returned to Jerusalem. One of these Jews was a man in Shushan named Mordecai. With him lived his cousin, a young woman named Esther. Mordecai had adopted her as his daughter when her parents died. Esther means "star" and she was as beautiful as her name. Esther was taken to the palace with other women of the empire. One of them would be chosen queen. There she was put under the care of Hegai.

Hegai liked Esther and helped her in the palace. Esther didn't tell Hegai that she was Jewish. In time, King Ahasuerus chose Esther over the others. At a grand banquet, Esther was made queen of Persia. When the king wanted to see Esther, he sent for her. No one could go to the king's rooms without an invitation. Not even the queen.

At that time, Mordecai was sitting at the palace gate. He overheard two men planning to kill the king. Mordecai sent word to Esther, who told Ahasuerus. The men were captured and punished by death. Mordecai had saved the king's life. This was written in the history of Ahasuerus's empire.

Find It in the Bible
ESTHER 2:5–23

HAMAN PLOTS AGAINST THE JEWS
PART ONE

King Ahasuerus gave a man named Haman power in the empire. The king allowed Haman to do whatever he wanted. The king even commanded that people bow to Haman when he passed. Everyone did this. Everyone but Mordecai, who only bowed to worship God.

Haman was outraged that Mordecai wouldn't bow down to him. But he felt he was too important to deal with one Jewish man. So Haman plotted to destroy all the Jews in the empire.

No one knew that Mordecai was Queen Esther's cousin. Nor was it known that Esther was a Jew.

Find It in the Bible
ESTHER 3:1–6

HAMAN PLOTS AGAINST THE JEWS
PART TWO

Haman spoke with King Ahasuerus. "Some people in your empire don't keep your laws. O king, you should command that the Jews be destroyed. I'll pay for putting them to death. The money will go into your treasury."

"Do whatever seems best to you," the king replied. So Haman wrote orders to every part of the empire.

"Destroy, kill, and wipe out all Jews," the orders read. "This includes young and old, women and children. Do this on one day: The thirteenth day of the twelfth month. Those who kill these people may take their property." Haman marked the orders with the king's stamp and sent them out. "Be ready for that day!" Haman ordered.

Haman and the king sat down to drink. But the city around them was restless. Mordecai heard of the law and went to the king's gate weeping. The Jews of the empire were in grief and mourning. Esther sent a servant to Mordecai to learn the news. Mordecai gave him a copy of the order with a message. "Take this to Esther," he said.

Find It in the Bible
ESTHER 3:7–4:8

"IF I DIE, I DIE"

Go to the king." Queen Esther read Mordecai's message. "Plead with him to save your people."

Esther returned a message: "No one can go to the king's rooms without an invitation, or they'll die."

Mordecai told Esther: "You'll be killed like all the other Jews. You may be silent, Esther, but God will rescue us another way. Who knows? Maybe you've become queen for just this time."

"Go then, Mordecai," wrote Esther. "Gather the Jews in Shushan. Pray for me three days. I'll do the same. Then I'll go into the king. If I die, I die."

Esther, dressed in her royal robes, stood in the king's court. The king, seeing her, held out the royal staff. This was his invitation. "What do you wish, Queen Esther? I'll give you anything."

"I've come to ask the king and Haman to dinner."

"Send word," he commanded. "Today Haman dines with the king and queen."

The three ate together. "What do you wish, Esther?" the king asked.

"Please, both of you, dine with me tomorrow. Then I'll tell you my desire."

Find It in the Bible
ESTHER 4:8–5:8

"HANG MORDECAI"

Haman went home boasting to his wife, Zeresh, of all his honors. "Even Queen Esther let only me dine with the king."

Then Haman became sour. "But all this does me no good. Mordecai refuses to bow down to me."

"Hang Mordecai," Zeresh suggested. "Then you can eat with the king and be happy." Haman liked this idea and ordered a tall gallows to be built. Mordecai would hang tomorrow.

That night, King Ahasuerus couldn't sleep, so he read the history of his empire. There he learned that Mordecai had saved his life. I wonder how I can honor this man, he thought. "What's the best way for me to honor a man, Haman?"

Haman thought the king wanted to honor him. "Give him your royal robes and your horse. Send a nobleman with him as he rides through the city. That man should shout, 'This is the man the king honors.'"

"Quickly, do this for Mordecai, the Jew," ordered the king. So Haman was the nobleman who shouted in Shushan: "Mordecai is the man the king honors."

Find It in the Bible
ESTHER 5:9–6:11

"THIS WICKED HAMAN!"

Your downfall has begun," Zeresh warned Haman. "If Mordecai is of the Jewish people, for sure you'll fall."

Soon the king and Haman went to Esther's banquet. "I'll give you anything," said the king. "I'll even give you half my kingdom."

"Let my life be spared," Esther answered. "And don't wipe out my people. We've been sold to be destroyed. No price can pay for this damage to your empire."

King Ahasuerus said to Queen Esther: "Who is he? Where is he that has imagined to do this?"

"A foe and enemy," Esther declared. "This wicked Haman!"

Find It in the Bible
ESTHER 6:12–7:6

THE JEWS CELEBRATE PURIM

The king left the banquet enraged. Haman threw himself on Esther's couch, begging for mercy. As he returned, the king saw this happening. "Look, he's attacking the queen!" the king said. Guards covered Haman's head. He was doomed.

"Look, there's the gallows," Harbona the guard spoke up. "Haman built it to hang Mordecai."

So they hanged Haman on his own gallows. That day, Ahasuerus gave Esther all of Haman's property. She told the king that Mordecai was her uncle. So the king gave Mordecai his ring. This ring had been on Haman's finger.

"O king," said Esther, "cancel the order to kill my people."

"Write an order," Ahasuerus answered. "Say what you please. Put my stamp on it. We'll send it by swift horses to all the empire."

So Mordecai wrote the order. It went to all 127 states in the empire, from India to Ethiopia.

A special festival called Purim was ordered by Queen Esther. The Jewish people celebrated their deliverance from death. To this day, at Purim, they tell the story of Esther and Mordecai.

Find It in the Bible
ESTHER 7:7–10:3

EZRA RETURNS TO JERUSALEM

Meanwhile, the Jews had been living in Judea for ninety years. Jerusalem was still a small town. Its houses were in ruins and it had no wall. The people were helpless against the desert bandits who robbed them.

In Babylon lived a Jewish priest and scribe named Ezra. He studied and kept God's law. He also taught the law. He gathered all the ancient writings. For the first time, the Old Testament books were all together. Ezra and other priests took these scrolls to Jerusalem.

There he found that some had married people who worshiped idols. Even the Jewish leaders had done this. Their children didn't know the Hebrew language or Israel's God. Ezra was horrified. He stopped eating and only prayed: "We have escaped and are only the leftovers of Israel. But our guilt has piled up to heaven. We cannot face you because of this."

While Ezra prayed, the people gathered around, sitting in heavy rain. Ezra sent away everyone who had married a foreigner. And so they left Jerusalem with their wives and children.

Find It in the Bible
EZRA 7:1–10:44

NEHEMIAH—THE CITY BUILDER

In the days of Ezra lived a Jewish man named Nehemiah. Nehemiah served wine to the Persian king Artaxerxes. But Nehemiah loved Jerusalem more than the king's palace. Once, when men came visiting from Judea, he asked, "How is Jerusalem?"

"The people are very poor," Nehemiah was told. "No one respects them. Jerusalem's wall is broken down and her gates are burned."

Later, Nehemiah wrote, "When I heard these words, I sat down and wept. I said, 'O great and awesome God, hear my prayer. You promised to gather your children to Jerusalem from under the farthest skies. O God, you bought them with your great power. I will speak to the king about this. Cause him to grant my request.'

"When I served the king his wine, he noticed I was sad. 'You aren't sick,' he said. 'So why are you sad?' I breathed a silent prayer.

" 'The city where my ancestors are buried is in ruins,' I answered.

" 'What is it you want?'

" 'Send me to Judea where my ancestors are buried. Let me rebuild the city.' The king was happy to send me to Jerusalem."

Find It in the Bible
NEHEMIAH 1:1–2:9

THE BUILDING BEGINS

Nehemiah and a group of horsemen rode one thousand miles to Jerusalem. He was there for three days. But Nehemiah told no one why God had sent him.

"I got up during the night," Nehemiah wrote. "A few men and I went out to look at the walls of Jerusalem. The way was too rough. So I left my horse and walked. The walls were in ruins and the gates burned to ash.

"I made my way back into the city. There I said, 'Come, let us rebuild the wall of Jerusalem. Then people around will respect us.' I told them what God had done with me. I also told them that the king had sent me. Then they said, 'Let's start building!'

"Soon people living in the lands around mocked us. 'What are you doing? Rebelling against the king?'

" 'The God of heaven will give us success,' I replied. 'We, his servants, are going to start building. You cannot share in this work.' "

Each family in Jerusalem agreed to build part of the wall. The high priest built one of the gates. A rich man built a long section. Others did a little. Some built much, some nothing.

Find It in the Bible
NEHEMIAH 2:11–3:32

THE BUILDING IS COMPLETED

Sanballat was a Samaritan. "What are these feeble Jews doing?" he mocked.

Tobiah, an Ammonite, stood with Sanballat. "Any fox running on that wall would break it down," he laughed.

The people of Jerusalem rebuilt the wall to half its height. The Arabians and the Ammonites and the Ashdodites were very angry. They didn't want the city to be strong.

The Jews set guards day and night and continued to work. "Don't be afraid of them," said Nehemiah. "Remember the Lord is great and awesome. Fight for your families and homes."

Sanballat and Tobiah saw they couldn't attack. So they sent Nehemiah a message: "Come down. Meet us in the valley of Ono." They wanted to kill Nehemiah there.

"I'm doing a great work," he replied. "Why should this work stop while I meet with you?"

Finally, fifty-two days after it began, the work was finished. The gates were closed and guards were posted. The enemies around were afraid. They knew that the work had been done with God's help.

Find It in the Bible
NEHEMIAH 4:1–6:16

DAY 209
EZRA READS THE LAW

Jerusalem's wall was built. The people of Israel safely settled into their towns and villages. With Ezra in Jerusalem, everyone gathered at the plaza by the Water Gate. "Bring the book of the law of Moses," they told Ezra.

When Ezra opened the book, the people stood. He blessed the Lord, and all the people answered, "Amen. Amen." From early morning until noon Ezra read to them. Listening carefully, the people wept when they heard the words of the law.

"This day is holy to the Lord," Ezra and the priests told them. "Don't mourn or weep." So the people returned to their homes to joyfully feast.

Nehemiah went back to Shushan and Persia's king. Later, he returned to Jerusalem. There he saw that people were working on the Sabbath. This is against God's law for the Jews. "What is this evil thing you're doing?" Nehemiah questioned. "How can you dishonor the Sabbath?"

He ordered that the city gates be closed at sunset before the Sabbath. They weren't opened until the morning after the Sabbath. Jerusalem began to grow and prosper as Jews returned there from all lands.

Find It in the Bible
NEHEMIAH 8:1–15:31

ZECHARIAH SEES AN ANGEL

Just before Jesus Christ was born, King Herod ruled Judea for the Roman Empire. Herod had rebuilt the ancient Jewish temple. There a priest helped with the worship. His name was Zechariah; his wife was Elizabeth.

One day, Zechariah was ministering in the Holy Place. Outside the court was full of worshipers. Suddenly, he saw an angel. Zechariah was terrified.

"Fear not," the angel said. "God has heard your prayer. Elizabeth will have a baby boy. You'll name him John. Many will rejoice when he's born. He'll have Elijah's spirit and turn many to the Lord."

"How will I know this is true?" questioned Zechariah. "I'm an old man and my wife is old, too."

"I'm Gabriel," said the angel. "God sent me to give you good news. But you don't believe me. I said that this will happen, but you won't speak until it does."

When Zechariah came out, the people could tell he'd seen a vision. He tried to signal to them, but they couldn't understand. When his service in the temple was over, Zechariah went home.

Find It in the Bible
Luke 1:1–23

GABRIEL GREETS MARY

This what God has done for me!" praised Elizabeth. She had just learned she and Zechariah were to have a baby.

Next, God sent the angel Gabriel to Nazareth. This town is in Galilee north of Judea. Living there was a girl named Mary, who was to wed Joseph.

"Greetings," Gabriel said. "You are God's favorite woman. God is with you."

"What kind of speaking is this?" Mary wondered.

"Don't be afraid," Gabriel continued. "You're going to have a baby boy. You'll call his name Jesus. He'll be called the Son of God."

Find It in the Bible
Luke 1:26–38

THE BIRTH OF JOHN THE BAPTIST

Hello, Elizabeth." Mary had come to see her cousin, Elizabeth. When Elizabeth heard Mary's voice, her baby jumped inside her. She was filled with the Holy Spirit.

"Mary! You are the most blessed of all women," Elizabeth exclaimed. "Your baby is blessed, too. Why has my Lord's mother come to see me? When I heard your voice, my baby jumped for joy inside me."

Some months later, Elizabeth's baby, John, was born. He would grow up in the wilderness—a Nazarite priest for God. This was the last prophet—John the Baptist.

Find It in the Bible
LUKE 1:39–80

THE BIRTH OF JESUS CHRIST

Joseph was a carpenter in Nazareth. He was soon to be Mary's husband. One night he had a dream. In it an angel spoke: "Joseph, take Mary as your wife. The child in her is from the Holy Spirit. When he's born, call him Jesus. He'll save his people from their sins."

In those days, Emperor Augustus Caesar commanded that his people be counted. To do this, everyone went to their hometown. For Mary and Joseph, this was Bethlehem. Bethlehem was also King David's hometown.

It was a long journey from Nazareth to Bethlehem. Mary, who was almost ready to have her baby, traveled with Joseph. They went down the hills in Galilee to the Jordan River. Then they followed the river to Judea. Up in the Judean hills, they came to Bethlehem. The town was full of people who had come to be counted. An inn was there, but it was full of people.

Suddenly, Mary had to give birth. So they went into a stable. Here Mary had her child, Jesus. She wrapped him in a blanket and put him to sleep in a feed trough.

Find It in the Bible
MATTHEW 1:18–21; LUKE 2:1–7

DAY 214
THE ANGEL'S ANNOUNCEMENT

That night, shepherds guarded their sheep near Bethlehem. Suddenly, they were surrounded with light. An angel stood there. The shepherds were terrified.

"Don't be afraid. I've come to give you good news. Today, in Bethlehem, Christ the Lord has been born. You'll find him wrapped in a blanket, sleeping in a feed trough."

Suddenly, the sky was filled with angels praising God. "Glory to God in heaven! On earth, peace and good will."

"Let's go to Bethlehem and see this wonderful thing."

And they did. There they found Mary, Joseph, and Jesus, as the angel had said.

Find It in the Bible
LUKE 2:8–20

THE PRAISE OF SIMEON

An old man named Simeon stood in the temple at Jerusalem. In his arms was the baby Jesus. Simeon praised God:

Thank you, Lord, for letting me leave this
*   life in peace.*
I've finally seen your salvation for all people.
He's a light so the Gentiles can see you;
And he's the glory of your people, Israel.

Mary and Joseph had brought Jesus to the temple. The law said they should promise him to God. The Spirit told Simeon to be there, too.

"Many in Israel will rise and fall because of him," Simeon told Jesus' parents.

Find It in the Bible
LUKE 2:21–35

THE RISING STAR OF CHRIST

In the East, far from Bethlehem, lived some very wise men who studied the stars. They traveled to Jerusalem to ask one question: "Where is the child who's born to be king of the Jews? We saw his star rise in the sky, so we came to honor him."

When King Herod heard this, he was afraid he would lose his kingdom. "Call the chief priests and scribes," he ordered. "They'll know where the Christ is to be born."

The Jewish priests explained to Herod the prophet Micah's words:

> *Bethlehem in Judea is one of your*
> *littlest towns.*
> *But out of her will come the ruler of Israel.*

Secretly, Herod spoke to the wise men from the East: "When you've found the child, tell me. I want to honor him, too."

When they had heard the king, the men set out. There, ahead of them, went the star they had seen rising. It stopped over a house in Bethlehem. The travelers were overcome by joy.

Find It in the Bible
MATTHEW 2:1–10

PRECIOUS GIFTS FOR JESUS

The joyous men entered the house and saw the child with Mary. They knelt down with reverence. Then, opening their treasure chests, they offered Jesus gifts. They gave him precious gold, frankincense, and myrrh.

When the men left, they didn't return to Herod. In a dream, one of them had been warned not to do this. So they traveled back to their land by another road.

Joseph saw an angel in a dream. "Hurry away to Egypt," the angel said. "Herod wants to kill the child."

That night the family left for Egypt.

Find It in the Bible
MATTHEW 2:11–14

CHRIST IS HIDDEN IN EGYPT

Herod was angry when he saw he'd been tricked by the wise men. He ordered his soldiers to kill all the babies in Bethlehem. He wanted to be sure he killed the king of the Jews.

Hundreds of years before, Jeremiah said this would happen:

I hear a voice in Ramah, near Bethlehem.
It is Rachel crying for her children.
She won't be comforted
because they are gone.

But Jesus was safe with his family in Egypt. When Herod died, an angel came to Joseph in a dream. "Get up and go back to Israel," the angel said. "Those who wanted to kill the child are dead." Long before, a prophet had spoken of this: "Out of Egypt I've called my son," he wrote.

But the family didn't return to Judea. Herod's son was ruling there, and Joseph was afraid. Again, he'd been warned in a dream. So Joseph took Mary and Jesus to Nazareth in Galilee. There they were safe. Another old prophet had seen this would happen. He said, "He will be called a Nazarene."

Find It in the Bible
MATTHEW 2:15–23

IN HIS FATHER'S HOUSE

Jesus grew and became strong. He was full of wisdom and God preferred him.

When Jesus was twelve years old, his family went to Jerusalem for the Passover. Afterward, they started home, but the boy Jesus stayed behind in Jerusalem. When they couldn't find him, they returned to Jerusalem. There they searched for Jesus.

After three days, they found him in the temple. The teachers were amazed at his understanding and answers. When his parents saw him, they were surprised. His mother said, "Child, why have you treated us like this? Your father and I have been looking for you. We've been worried sick."

"Why were you searching for me?" Jesus asked her. "Didn't you know that I would be in my Father's house?" But they didn't understand his meaning.

Then Jesus went down with them from Jerusalem. They retuned to Nazareth and he obeyed them. His mother always remembered the things he did and said.

Jesus grew in wisdom and in years. He was preferred by God and the people.

Find It in the Bible
LUKE 2:40–52

THE WORK OF JOHN THE BAPTIST

John, the son of Elizabeth and Zechariah, lived in the wilderness. Zechariah's son was also Israel's last prophet. When he was thirty, God sent him to the Jewish people. He told them to turn from sin and be forgiven. John baptized those who turned from sin in the Jordan River.

Earlier the prophet Isaiah spoke of John the Baptist:

His voice is crying in the wilderness.
He will go ahead of the Lord to
*   make the paths straight for him.*
Then everyone will see God's salvation.

John the Baptist wore rough clothes woven from camel's hair and a leather belt. He ate dried grasshoppers and wild honey from the trees. John's words were different, too. He said: "Turn from sin and do right. The kingdom of heaven is nearby. Its king will soon be here."

Pharisees were men of Israel who made a show of being good. John told them, "You're the children of snakes. Who told you to escape from God's anger against you?"

Find It in the Bible
LUKE 3:1–14

JOHN BAPTIZES JESUS

I wonder if he's Christ?" everyone wondered about John the Baptist.

"I baptize you with water," he answered. "The one who's coming is greater than I am. He'll baptize you with the Holy Spirit and fire." John was speaking of Jesus.

Jesus came to be baptized by John. But John said, "You should baptize me."

"It's proper for us to do this," Jesus answered. "We'll be doing what's right."

John baptized Jesus. Just then, God's Spirit came down like a dove. And God spoke: "This is my Son whom I love. He pleases me."

Find It in the Bible
LUKE 3:15–22; MATTHEW 3:13–17

THE DEVIL TEMPTS JESUS

The Spirit of God led Jesus into the wilderness. There he was tempted by the devil. When he was hungry, the devil came. "If you're God's Son, make these stones into bread."

"One doesn't only live on bread. God's words are food as well."

The devil took him to the temple roof. "The angels won't let you get hurt," he tempted. "So jump to the ground."

"It's written, 'Don't put God to the test.' "

"I'll give you all of earth's kingdoms; worship me!" commanded Satan.

"Get away, Satan! The Bible says, 'Worship and serve only God.' "

Find It in the Bible
LUKE 4:1–13

JESUS FINDS HIS FOLLOWERS

When the devil left Jesus alone, angels came and cared for him. Then he went back to where John was by the Jordan River. John saw Jesus coming toward him. "Look! It's the Lamb of God who takes away the world's sin. This is the one I said was greater than I am. I've seen this, and now I tell you: This is the Son of God!"

The next morning, John was standing with two of his followers. Jesus walked by. John shouted, "Look, here is the Lamb of God!" His two followers heard this and followed Jesus.

Jesus turned around and said, "What are you looking for?"

"Teacher," they replied, "where do you live?"

"Come and see."

One man, Andrew, found his brother, Simon, and said, "We've found the Christ!" He brought Simon to Jesus.

Jesus looked at Simon and said, "You are John's son, Simon. But your new name is Peter."

The next day, Jesus went to Galilee. He said to Philip, "Follow me."

Later, Jesus met Nathaniel, who said: "Teacher, you're the Son of God! You're the King of Israel!"

Find It in the Bible
JOHN 1:29–51

DAY 224
"YOU'LL FISH FOR PEOPLE"

Jesus walked by the Sea of Galilee. There he saw Peter and Andrew again. They were casting a net into the sea because they were fishermen. He said to them, "Follow me and you'll fish for people."

Right away, they left their nets and followed him. Farther down the beach, Jesus saw two other brothers. James and John were in a fishing boat with their father, Zebedee. They were mending their nets. Jesus called to them. At once, they left their father in the boat and followed him.

Find It in the Bible
MATTHEW 4:18–22

THE MIRACLE AT THE WEDDING

Jesus and his followers went to a town called Cana. There was a wedding in that town. Everyone was having fun and eating a big meal. But before the meal was over, they ran out of wine. Mary, Jesus' mother, knew he could help. Mary said to Jesus, "They have no wine." He said, "It is not time for me to do miracles." But Mary told the people, "Do what he tells you."

Six big stone jars were standing there. They each held as much water as a bathtub. Jesus said, "Fill those jars with water." The servants did what he said. Then Jesus told them, "Take some of it to the leader of this wedding." So they dipped some water out of the jars. It had changed to wine.

The leader of the wedding was surprised. He spoke to the bridegroom. "This wine is better than any you have served so far. You kept the best wine until last."

This was the first time Jesus did something to prove he was the Son of God. When his followers saw it, they believed in Jesus even more.

Find It in the Bible
JOHN 2:1–11

CLEANSING HIS FATHER'S HOUSE

Jesus went up to Jerusalem for the Passover. In the temple, he found people selling sheep and doves for sacrifices. There were money changers at their tables. Jesus made a whip out of cords. He used it to drive these people out of the temple. He chased their sheep into the street and poured out their coins.

"Take these things out of here!" he shouted. "Stop making my Father's house a marketplace!"

The Jews said to him, "What right do you have to do this? Show us a sign that God's given you control of the temple."

"Here's your sign," Jesus said. "Destroy this temple and in three days I'll raise it up."

"It's taken forty-six years to build this temple. It's not finished yet," the Jews said. "Will you raise it up in three days?"

But Jesus wasn't talking about that temple on Mount Moriah. He was speaking of the temple of his body. They would put him to death. But he would come back from death in three days. His followers remembered that he'd said this. So when Jesus returned from death, they believed his words.

Find It in the Bible
JOHN 2:13–22

"I'LL BE LIFTED UP ON A CROSS"

Nicodemus visited Jesus at night. He was a Pharisee and a leader of the Jews. "We know you're a teacher from God," he said. "No one can do these things unless God is with him."

"I'll tell you the truth," Jesus answered. "No one can see God's kingdom without being born of the Spirit."

"How can an old man be born again?"

"Whatever is born of a woman is human. Whatever is born of the Spirit is spirit."

"How can this be?" Nicodemus wondered.

"Are you a teacher of Israel?" Jesus asked. "Yet you don't understand?" Then Jesus said: "Remember how Moses lifted up a brass serpent on a pole? Whoever saw it was healed of the snakes' poison."

"Yes," said Nicodemus.

"Well, I'm the Son of Man. I'll be lifted up on a cross. Whoever believes in me will be healed of sin and have eternal life. Because God loved the world so much that he gave his only Son, whoever believes in him won't die forever. They'll have eternal life."

Find It in the Bible
JOHN 3:1–21

THE WOMAN AT JACOB'S WELL

PART ONE

Jesus traveled from Judea to Samaria. About noontime, Jesus rested by Jacob's well, and his followers went to buy food.

A woman came to the well to draw water. "Give me a drink," Jesus said.

"You're a Jew," she said. "I'm a Samaritan. Jews don't share with Samaritans."

"You don't know who's asking you for a drink. If you did, you'd ask me for a drink. Then I'd give you living water."

"You don't have a bucket, sir. How will you get that living water?"

"Whoever drinks water from this well," Jesus said, "will get thirsty again. But when I give you water the well is inside of you. It bubbles up to give you eternal life."

"Sir," the woman said, "please give me this water. Then I'll never thirst again. I won't have to come to this well."

"Go get your husband and come back."

"I don't have a husband."

"What you say is true," Jesus said. "You've had five husbands. And the man you have now isn't your husband."

Find It in the Bible
JOHN 4:3–18

DAY 229
THE WOMAN AT JACOB'S WELL
PART TWO

The Samaritan woman said, "I see you're a prophet. Tell me, which is right, to worship at this mountain or at Jerusalem?"

"Believe me," Jesus answered. "The time has come when you won't worship the Father in either place. The real worshipers worship the Father in spirit and in truth. God is seeking people who will worship him this way. You see, God is Spirit. So the people who worship him must worship in spirit and truth."

Then the woman said, "I know Christ is coming. When he does, he'll teach us everything."

"I'm speaking to you. I'm Christ."

Just then, Jesus' followers came back with the food. They were surprised that Jesus was talking with this Samaritan woman. She left her water jug at the well and hurried back to town. "Come and see a man who told me everything I've ever done! Could he be Christ?"

Many people in that town believed in Jesus because of the woman. Jesus stayed there two days. Many more believed because they heard his words.

Find It in the Bible
JOHN 4:19–42

A NOBLEMAN'S HOUSEHOLD BELIEVES

When Jesus got back to Galilee, the people welcomed him. They had seen what he'd done in Jerusalem. Jesus went to Cana, where he changed the water into wine. In nearby Capernaum, there was a nobleman whose son was sick. He had heard that Jesus had come from Judea. This man went up the hills from the seashore to see Jesus. He begged him: "Come and heal my son. He's about to die."

"Unless you see miracles you won't believe," Jesus replied.

The nobleman said, "Sir, come down before my little boy dies."

"Go; your son will live."

The man believed Jesus' words and started for home. The next day, his slaves met him on the way. "Your child is alive!" they exclaimed.

He asked them what time the boy began to get well. "Yesterday at one in the afternoon his fever went down." That was the exact hour that Jesus said, "Your son will live." So the nobleman believed as did all his household.

This was the second time Jesus did something to prove he was the Son of God.

Find It in the Bible
JOHN 4:45–54

TROUBLE IN NAZARETH

Jesus went back to his hometown of Nazareth. In the synagogue, Jesus stood up to read from the sixty-first chapter of Isaiah:

The Spirit of the Lord is upon me. I'm anointed to bring good news to the poor. He has sent me to call out "freedom!" to the captives and give sight to the blind; to let the overloaded people go free; and to proclaim the year of God's grace to everyone.

Then Jesus rolled up the scroll and handed it back. Everyone was looking at him. He said, "Today these words have come true." Everyone was amazed at his gracious words.

But then someone said, "Isn't this Joseph's son? We know his brothers and sisters. How can he teach us?"

Jesus said, "You're thinking: 'Why doesn't he do miracles like he did in Capernaum?' I'll tell you the truth. A prophet is never welcome in his hometown."

Find It in the Bible
Luke 4:16–24

TROUBLE IN NAZARETH
PART TWO

I'll tell you the truth. A prophet is never welcome in his hometown." Jesus was speaking with the people in the synagogue in Nazareth.

"In Elijah's time, it didn't rain for three and a half years. There were many widows in Israel. But which widow did God tell Elijah to help? A woman who was outside of Israel; not a Jew. And weren't there many lepers in Israel in Elisha's time? But the only leper the prophet healed was Naaman from Syria."

When they heard this, everyone in the synagogue was enraged. They wanted miracles like in Capernaum. They got up and drove Jesus out of town. Nazareth was built on a hillside. They led him up to the top of the highest hill. They wanted to throw him off the cliff. But Jesus slipped away from them and went on his way. It wasn't yet time for him to die.

In Capernaum by the Sea of Galilee, Jesus taught the next Sabbath day. They were amazed at his teaching. Unlike other teachers, Jesus spoke like an expert.

Find It in the Bible
LUKE 4:24–32

"YOU'RE THE SON OF GOD!"

In Capernaum lived a man who was controlled by a demon. He saw Jesus, and the demon cried out: "Let us alone, Jesus of Nazareth! Have you come to destroy us? I know you; you're the Holy One of God."

Jesus commanded the demon, "Be silent and come out of him!" The demon threw the man down on the ground and came out. The man wasn't hurt.

Everyone around was amazed. "What kind of speaking is this?" they wondered. "He has power to command the evil spirits. And out they come!" The reports about Jesus were heard everywhere.

After this, Jesus entered Peter's house. There, Peter's mother-in-law was suffering with a high fever. They asked him about her. Jesus stood over the woman and rebuked the fever. It left her. Right away, Peter's mother-in-law got out of bed. She served them their meal.

As the sun was setting, people brought the sick to Jesus. He put his hands on them and cured them. Demons came out of many people, shouting, "You're the Son of God!" Jesus wouldn't let the demons speak because they knew he was Christ.

Find It in the Bible
LUKE 4:33–41

"LET DOWN YOUR NETS FOR FISH"

Once Jesus was beside the Sea of Galilee. Nearby were two fishing boats, belonging to Peter and Andrew and James and John. These young disciples were nearby washing their nets. Jesus stepped into Peter's boat and sat teaching the crowds.

Jesus finished teaching. "Peter," he said, "put out into deep water and let down your nets for fish."

"Master," Peter answered, "we've worked all night long and caught nothing. But if you say so, I'll let down the nets." When they did, they caught so many fish their nets were breaking. Peter signaled James and John, who came and filled both boats to overflowing!

Overwhelmed with God's wonder, he fell down and cried, "Go away from me, Lord. I'm a sinful man!"

"Don't be afraid," Jesus comforted Peter. "From now on, you'll catch people." The young men left their boats and all they had and followed Jesus.

Find It in the Bible
LUKE 5:1–11

"BE MADE CLEAN"

In one city was a man covered with leprosy. When he saw Jesus, he bowed to the ground. "If you choose," he begged, "you can make me clean."

"I do choose this," Jesus said. "Be made clean." Instantly, the leprosy was gone. Jesus ordered him to tell no one. "Show the priest and make an offering to God."

But more than ever the news about Jesus spread. People were amazed when they heard him. Crowds would gather to listen and be healed of disease. Sometimes Jesus would get away to secluded places and pray.

Find It in the Bible
LUKE 5:12–16

THE POWER TO FORGIVE SINS

Pharisees and teachers came from every village in Galilee. They came all the way from Jerusalem to Capernaum. Jesus was teaching them, and God's power was with him to heal. Just then, men came carrying a paralyzed man on a bed. They tried to bring him into the house to Jesus. But it was too crowded. So they went up on the roof and took off some roof tiles. They let the paralyzed man down into the house. There he was in front of Jesus in the middle of the crowd.

Jesus saw that these men had faith. "Friend," he said, "your sins are forgiven you."

The Pharisees questioned this. "He's speaking heresy," they whispered. "No one can forgive sins except God."

Jesus knew their thoughts. "Why do you question this? Is it easier to say: 'Your sins are forgiven,' or 'Stand up and walk?' I want you to know that I have the power to forgive sins." Then Jesus spoke to the paralyzed man: "Stand up, take your bed, and go home." And the man did this, praising God.

Everyone was amazed and praised God. "We've seen great things today," they said.

Find It in the Bible
Luke 5:17–26

JESUS IGNORES THE SABBATH
PART ONE

Jesus went up to the Passover festival. There, near the sheep gate, is a pool called Bethesda. Many blind, lame, and paralyzed people waited there for the water to bubble up because of its healing power.

Jesus asked a man who'd been sick for thirty-eight years if he wanted to be made well.

"Someone always gets into the pool ahead of me."

Jesus said, "Stand up, take your mat, and walk." Instantly, the man was healed, picked up his mat, and walked away.

Someone said, "Today's the Sabbath. It's against the law to carry that mat."

"The man who healed me said to pick up my mat."

"Who was that?" the Pharisees asked.

"I don't know."

Jesus had left the area. Later, when the man saw Jesus in the temple, he told the Pharisees, and they harassed Jesus because of the Sabbath healing.

"My Father works every day, and so do I," Jesus replied. The Pharisees wanted to kill Jesus for this. He'd made himself the same as God.

Find It in the Bible
JOHN 5:1–18

JESUS IGNORES THE SABBATH

PART TWO

Jesus went into the synagogue on the Sabbath. There was a man who had a disabled hand. The people wondered if he would heal on the Sabbath. Jesus asked them, "Is it against the law to do good on the Sabbath? What about to do harm? Does your law allow me to save a life on the Sabbath? How about to kill?" They didn't answer.

"Stretch out your hand," he said to the man. The hand was healed. Right away, the Pharisees plotted with the Romans to destroy Jesus.

Find It in the Bible
MARK 3:1–6

DAY 239
JESUS TEACHES ON THE MOUNTAIN

Jesus saw the huge crowds on the mountain. His disciples, too, came, and he taught them:

*The poor in spirit are blessed because
    theirs is the kingdom of heaven.
The meek are blessed because they'll
    inherit the earth.
People who are hungry to do right are
    blessed because they'll be filled.
People who have mercy are blessed
    because they'll be given mercy.
The pure in heart are blessed because
    they'll see God.
Peacemakers are blessed because they'll be
    called children of God.*

Find It in the Bible
MATTHEW 5:1–9

THE FAITH OF A CENTURION

In Capernaum lived an officer of the Roman army. He was called a centurion because he led one hundred men. As a Roman, he was a foreigner in Israel. The Jews called foreigners and non-Jews "Gentiles." So this centurion was a Gentile. He had a favorite servant who was nearly dying. The centurion sent for Jesus: "Ask him to come and heal my slave," he said.

"This centurion deserves your help," they told Jesus. "He loves our people and paid for the building of our synagogue."

Not far from the man's house, friends of the centurion met Jesus. "The centurion sent this message," they said. " 'Lord, don't trouble yourself. I don't deserve to have you in my house. If you simply speak the words, my servant will be healed. I'm like you, Lord; someone else tells me what to do. Then I give orders to my soldiers and servants.' "

Jesus was amazed that the centurion said this. He spoke to the crowd: "I haven't found this kind of faith in all of Israel."

When the centurion's friends returned, the servant was healed.

Find It in the Bible
LUKE 7:1–10

DAY 241
THE FUNERAL AT NAIN

Jesus and his disciples went to the town of Nain. A large crowd followed. There, a funeral procession came out of the town's gate. A young man had died. His mother, a widow, followed his body, weeping. A large crowd from the town was there.

The Lord saw her and had pity. "Don't weep," he said and stopped the procession. Then he said, "Young man, I say to you, get up!" The man sat up and began to speak. Jesus gave him to his mother.

The crowds were afraid. "A great prophet has come to us," they declared.

Find It in the Bible
LUKE 7:11–16

DAY 242
SINS AND LOVE
PART ONE

A Pharisee named Simon invited Jesus to supper. There, a woman came with a beautiful little jar of perfume. She was weeping at Jesus' feet. This was a well-known sinful woman who lived in town. Jesus' feet were bathed in her tears. Then the woman dried them with her hair. As this sinful woman kissed Jesus' feet, she anointed them with perfume.

"I don't think this man's a prophet," Simon said to himself. "If he were, he'd know who's touching him. She's a sinner."

Find It in the Bible
LUKE 7:36–39

DAY 243
SINS AND LOVE
PART TWO

Jesus spoke up. "Simon, I want to tell you a story.

"Two people owed another man money. The first owed five hundred dollars. The other owed fifty dollars. Neither of them could pay. So he told them both they didn't need to pay him back. Which one loved him more?"

Simon the Pharisee answered, "I suppose the one who owed the most money."

Jesus said to him, "You're right. I came to your house. Did you give me water to wash my feet? No. Do you see this woman, Simon? She bathed my feet in tears and wiped them with her hair. You didn't greet me with a kiss. But since I came, she hasn't stopped kissing my feet. You didn't anoint my head with oil. But she has anointed my feet. I tell you, her many sins are forgiven. But the one who's done little to forgive loves little."

Jesus said to the woman, "Your sins are forgiven."

The people around the table murmured. "Who's this who forgives sins?"

And he said to the woman, "Your faith has saved you; go in peace."

Find It in the Bible

Luke 7:40–50

THE SEEDS OF GOD'S WORD

A great crowd gathered, and Jesus taught them with a story: "A farmer was planting seeds. As he spread the seeds, some fell on the path. Birds ate these seeds. Some seeds fell in with rocks. They died because there wasn't enough water. Seeds fell into the weeds and couldn't grow. Others fell into good soil. These seeds grew and gave the farmer a good crop."

Later, Jesus told his disciples, "The seeds are God's word. The ones that fell on the path mean this: Some people hear God's word. Then the devil takes it from their heart. So they can't believe and be saved.

"The seeds in the rocks are the people who happily believe for a little while. But in hard times, they forget God's word.

"The seeds in the weeds mean this: Some people hear God's word and go on their way. The word can't grow because their heart is full of other things.

"Then there are the seeds in good soil. These show God's word in a good heart. That person's life is changed forever."

Find It in the Bible
LUKE 8:4–15

THE WIND AND THE SEA OBEY HIM

At evening, Jesus said, "Let's cross to the other side." With other boats, the disciples rowed across the Sea of Galilee. A big storm came up. Waves beat into the boat. It was about to be swamped. But Jesus was asleep in the stern of the boat.

They awakened him. "Teacher, don't you care that we're all about to drown?"

He woke up and rebuked the wind. Speaking to the sea, Jesus said, "Peace! Be still." The wind stopped, and there was dead calm on the water.

"Why are you afraid?" he asked them. "Do you still have no faith?"

They were filled with great awe. "Who is this?" they asked each other. "Even the wind and the sea obey him."

They came to the other side of the sea. This was the country of the Gerasenes. A man lived in a graveyard here. He howled on the mountainsides and bruised himself with stones. An unclean spirit lived in this man. Whenever he was captured and chained, he broke the chains and escaped.

This man with an unclean spirit saw Jesus arrive at the shore.

Find It in the Bible
MARK 4:35–5:6

THE MAN OF UNCLEAN SPIRITS

The man with the unclean spirit spied Jesus. He screamed and shouted: "What do you have to do with me, Jesus, Son of the Most High God?"

"Come out of him, you unclean spirit!" Jesus commanded.

"I beg you in God's name, don't make me suffer," it answered.

"What's your name?" Jesus asked the spirit.

"It's Legion because there are many of us in this man. Please, don't send us away."

Nearby grazed a herd of pigs. "Let us enter into the pigs," the spirits begged. Jesus gave them permission. The legion of spirits came out of the man, entering the pigs, and all of the animals rushed down the hill and into the sea.

People found the man of unclean spirits fully clothed and sitting in his right mind with Jesus. They were afraid and pleaded with Jesus, "Go away!"

Before leaving, Jesus spoke to the man. "Go home. Tell your friends how much the Lord has done for you." The man went to ten cities telling what Jesus had done.

Find It in the Bible
MARK 5:6–20

"WHO TOUCHED ME?"

Again they crossed the sea in the boat. On the other shore, a big crowd gathered. A Jewish leader named Jairus came forward and fell at his feet. "My little daughter is about to die. Come and touch her so she will live." So Jesus went with him. The crowd followed and pushed in on him.

In the crowd was a woman who'd been bleeding for twelve years. She had spent all her money on doctors. They couldn't help her; in fact, she grew worse. She'd heard about Jesus and came up behind him. She said to herself, "If I touch his clothes, I'll be healed." She touched his cloak. Instantly, her bleeding stopped. The woman knew she was healed.

Jesus also knew something had happened. He had felt power go out from him. "Who touched me?" he asked.

"The crowd is pushing in on you," said his disciples. "How can you ask, 'Who touched me?' " But he looked all around for who had done it.

The woman came to him in fear and trembling. She told him the whole story. "Daughter," he said, "your faith has made you well. Go in peace and be healed."

Find It in the Bible
MARK 5:21–34

DAY 248
"SHE'S NOT DEAD; SHE'S SLEEPING"

Your daughter's dead, Jairus," people said. "Don't trouble the teacher." But Jesus overheard.

"Don't fear, Jairus," he said. "Only believe."

Jesus wouldn't let anyone follow him to Jairus' house. Only Peter, James, and John went along. There, people loudly wailed.

"Why so much noise? She's not dead; she's sleeping." They laughed at Jesus. He put them outside. With her parents and the disciples, Jesus went to the girl. He took her hand. "Little girl, get up." She arose and walked around. They were overcome with amazement. "Don't tell anyone," Jesus ordered. "And give her something to eat."

Find It in the Bible

MARK 5:35–43

THE DEATH OF JOHN THE BAPTIST

King Herod was wicked and confused. He had married his brother's wife, Herodias. When John the Baptist heard this, he said, "That's against the law." So Herod put John in prison. He was afraid to kill him because John was honored as a prophet.

On Herod's birthday, they held a feast. Herodias's daughter danced, and Herod was happy with her. "I'll give you anything you want," he promised.

Her mother told her, "Ask for John the Baptist's head on a plate." And she did. The king was troubled about this. But everyone had heard his promise. So he sent guards to cut off John's head. It was given to the girl, who gave it to Herodias.

Jesus had talked to his disciples about John: "He was more than a prophet. He is the man the prophet Malachi wrote about: 'Look, I'm sending my messenger ahead of you. He will prepare a way for you.' John did this for me.

"No one ever born was greater than John the Baptist. But the littlest in the kingdom of heaven is greater than he is. He heard that the good news was coming. Now the good news is yours."

Find It in the Bible
MATTHEW 14:1–12; 11:7–15

DAY 250
JESUS FEEDS THE CROWDS

Jesus heard John the Baptist had been killed. So he retreated in a boat to a secluded place. The people followed on foot around the Sea of Galilee. So when Jesus came ashore, he saw huge crowds waiting. There he cared for them.

"It's late," said the disciples. "Send them away for food."

"They don't need to leave," said Jesus. "You give them food."

"All we have is five loaves and two fish."

Taking these, Jesus looked up to heaven. He blessed and broke the loaves. Then everyone ate their fill. They filled twelve baskets with leftovers.

Find It in the Bible
MATTHEW 14:13–21

JESUS WALKS ON THE SEA

After feeding the crowds, Jesus sent the disciples back to the boat. He went up the mountain alone to pray. By evening, the boat was far from land. The disciples struggled to sail against high waves and strong winds. At dawn, Jesus came to them walking on the sea.

"It's a ghost!" they cried out in fear.

"Take heart, it is I," Jesus said. "Don't be afraid."

Peter answered, "Lord, command me to walk on the water."

He said, "Come."

So Peter started walking on the water toward Jesus. But when Peter felt the wind, he began sink. Peter cried out, "Lord, save me!"

Instantly, Jesus reached and caught him. "You have so little faith," Jesus said. "Why did you doubt?" Back in the boat, the wind stopped.

"Truly you are the Son of God," they said. And the disciples worshiped him.

When the boat came to land, the sick were brought to Jesus. "Just let us touch the edge of your cloak," the people begged. All those who touched it were healed.

Find It in the Bible
MATTHEW 14:22–36

DAY 252
JESUS—THE BREAD OF LIFE

Jesus told the crowd, "You want me because I fed you yesterday. But hunger for food that gives you eternal life. I'll give you this food."

"What good works can we do for God?" they asked.

"Believe in the one that God has sent."

They said, "when we see a miracle we'll believe in you. Our ancestors ate manna from heaven. What are you going to do for us?"

"My Father has given you real bread from heaven. God's bread is the one he's sent to give the world life."

"Sir," they pleaded, "always give us this bread."

Then Jesus said to them, "I'm the bread of life. Whoever comes to me will never be hungry. Whoever believes in me will never be thirsty.

"Your ancestors ate the manna, and still they died. I'm the living bread that came down from heaven. Whoever eats this bread will live forever."

Some of his disciples complained about this teaching and left him.

"Will you leave, too?" Jesus asked.

"Where will we go?" answered Peter. "You have the words of eternal life."

Find It in the Bible
JOHN 6:25–68

DAY 253
A GENTILE DOG AND
THE BREAD OF LIFE

Leaving Capernaum and traveling north, Jesus came to Tyre and Sidon, a place where Gentiles lived. A Canaanite woman shouted, "Have mercy on me, Lord, Son of David! My daughter is harassed by a demon."

His disciples urged him, "Send her away."

She came and knelt down. "Lord, help me."

"It wouldn't be fair," he answered. "I can't throw Israel's bread to the Gentile dogs."

"That's true, Lord," she said. "But little dogs get the crumbs that fall from their master's table."

"Woman, you have great faith! You may have what you wish." And her daughter was healed instantly.

After this, Jesus journeyed back along the Sea of Galilee. He went up a mountainside and sat down. Huge crowds came with the lame, the blind, the mute, and others. They were brought to him, and he cured them. The crowd was amazed. They saw the mute speaking, the lame walking, and the blind seeing. And they praised the God of Israel.

Find It in the Bible
MATTHEW 15:21–31

"WHO DO PEOPLE SAY I AM?"

At Caesarea Philippi, Jesus asked his disciples, "Who do people say I am?"

"Some say you're John the Baptist. Others say Elijah. Still others think you're Jeremiah or one of the prophets."

He said to them, "Who do you say that I am?"

Peter spoke up. "You're the Christ, the Son of the living God."

"You're blessed, Peter," said Jesus. "No man told you this. My Father in heaven has shown it to you. This is the rock on which I'll build my church. You, Peter, are a stone in that building. And the church I'll build is stronger than the gates of hell." He sternly told them, "Don't tell anyone I'm the Christ."

He began to tell his disciples what would soon happen: "I'll go to Jerusalem. There I'll suffer and be killed. Three days later, I'll return from death."

"God forbid it, Lord," declared Peter. "This must never happen to you!"

Jesus rebuked Peter. "If you think that way, you'll block my plans. Your words are from Satan. You see me as a human king. Instead, you must understand: God sent me so that these things could happen."

Find It in the Bible
MATTHEW 16:13–23

THE VOICE ON THE MOUNTAINTOP

Six days later, Jesus took Peter, James, and John to the mountaintop. There Jesus was changed. His face shone like the sun. His clothes became dazzling. Suddenly, Moses and Elijah appeared and spoke with Jesus.

Peter said, "Shall we pitch three tents? One to worship you, one to worship Moses, and one for Elijah?" Peter was talking when a bright cloud covered them.

A voice spoke from the cloud, "This is my beloved Son. He pleases me. Listen to him!" The disciples fell to the ground in fear. When they looked up, only Jesus was there.

Find It in the Bible
MATTHEW 17:1–8

NOTHING IS IMPOSSIBLE WITH FAITH

Jesus and the three disciples came down the mountain to the crowd. A man knelt down in front of Jesus. "Lord, have mercy on my son. An evil spirit controls him; he suffers terribly. Sometimes he falls into the fire. Other times he falls into the water. I brought him to your disciples, but they couldn't cure him."

Jesus said, "You people have no faith. You're so corrupt. How much longer do I have to put up with you? Bring the boy to me." Jesus rebuked the demon and it came out. The boy was cured instantly.

The disciples took him aside and asked, "Why couldn't we do that?"

"Because you have so little faith. You could do so much with just a tiny bit of faith. Faith the size of a mustard seed can move a mountain into the sea. With faith, nothing would be impossible for you."

They were all living in Galilee. There Jesus told them, "I am going to be trapped and sold to men in Jerusalem. They will kill me. Three days later, I'll return from death." These words upset and worried the disciples.

Find It in the Bible
MATTHEW 17:14–23

THE GREATEST IN THE KINGDOM

In Capernaum, the time had come to collect the temple tax. The tax collectors came to Peter. "Does Jesus pay the tax?" they asked.

"Yes, he does," Peter answered.

When Peter came home, Jesus asked him this question: "From whom do kings collect taxes? Do they take the money from their own children or from others?"

"From others," Peter answered.

"Then the king's children don't pay the temple tax. However, we don't want to trouble the tax collectors. Go to the sea and cast in a hook. Pull in the first fish you hook. When you open its mouth, you'll find a coin. Take that and give it to them. It will pay your tax and mine."

Then the disciples asked Jesus a question: "Which of us will be greatest in the kingdom of heaven?"

Jesus called to a little child. "I'll tell you the truth. Do you want to enter the kingdom? Then you'll have to change and become like a little child. Anyone who is humble like this child is greatest in the kingdom. Anyone who welcomes such a child welcomes me."

Find It in the Bible
MATTHEW 17:24–18:5

"FORGIVE OTHERS FROM YOUR HEART"

Peter asked, "How often should I forgive someone? Seven times?"

Jesus answered, "Not seven times; I tell you: seventy-seven times.

"Once a king's servant owed him ten million dollars. He couldn't pay. The king ordered, 'Sell this man and his family into slavery to pay his debt.'

"The servant begged, 'Be patient. I'll pay you everything.'

"Pitying him, the king said, 'You don't have to pay.'

"Later, a man owed him one hundred dollars. 'Pay me what you owe,' he demanded. The man pleaded, 'Have patience. I'll pay you!' But the servant put him in jail until he could pay.

"Other servants saw this and told the king. The king said to the servant, 'You wicked servant, I forgave you your debt because you begged me to. I had mercy on you. Shouldn't you have had mercy on that man?' The king sent him to prison until he'd paid his debt.

"Peter, the lesson is this: My Father is like the king in this story. You are like the servant. So always forgive others from your heart."

Find It in the Bible
MATTHEW 18:21–35

THE CAMEL IN THE NEEDLE'S EYE

Later, a young man asked, "What shall I do to have eternal life?" "Keep the commandments," Jesus answered.

"I've kept all ten. What else is there?"

"Sell everything. Give the money to the poor. Come and follow me."

When the young man heard this, he sadly walked away. He was very rich.

Jesus spoke to his disciples: "Can a camel go through a needle's eye? That's how hard it is for the rich to enter the kingdom."

"So who can be saved?" they wondered.

"To you, it's impossible," he answered. "But God can do anything."

Find It in the Bible
MATTHEW 19:16–26

THE ONE THING THAT'S NEEDED

One day Jesus went to Martha and Mary's house. Mary had once anointed Jesus' feet and wiped them with her hair. She enjoyed sitting at the Lord's feet listening to him talk. Martha was very busy with other things in the house. She said to Jesus, "My sister has left all the work for me to do. Does that bother you at all?"

"Martha, Martha," he answered, "you're worried about so many things. But there's only one thing that's really needed. Mary has chosen to love me, and that won't be taken from her."

Find It in the Bible
LUKE 10:38–42

MUD ON A BLIND MAN'S EYES

PART ONE

A s Jesus walked in Jerusalem, he saw a blind man. This man had been born blind. His disciples asked this question: "Teacher, whose fault was it that he is blind? Did his parents sin? Was it his sin that caused this?"

"He was born blind for a reason," Jesus answered. "This has nothing to do with anyone's sin. God wants to work in him. We must do God's work while it is day. Night is coming when no one can work. As long as I'm in the world, I'm the light of the world."

Then Jesus spit on the ground. He made mud with his spit and spread it on the man's eyes. "Go wash your eyes in the Siloam pool," Jesus told him.

The blind man went to the pool with mud on his eyes. He washed, and for the first time in his life, he could see. His neighbors had always seen him begging. "Isn't this the man who used to sit and beg?" they asked.

"It's the same man," some said.

"No," others said. "This man just looks like him."

He told them, "I'm the same man."

Find It in the Bible
JOHN 9:1–9

MUD ON A BLIND MAN'S EYES
PART TWO

The once-blind beggar tried to explain why he could see: "Jesus spread the mud on my eyes and said 'Wash at Siloam Pool.'"

Because it was the Sabbath, they brought the man to the Pharisees. "This man isn't from God," some Pharisees said.

"But how could a sinner do this miracle?" others asked. The Pharisees couldn't agree. So they asked the blind beggar, "What do you think? He gave you your sight."

"He's a prophet."

The Pharisees didn't believe him. "He was never blind," they said. So they asked his parents.

"This is our son," they said. "He was born blind. We don't know why he can now see. He's a grown man. Ask him." So the Pharisees called the man for the second time.

"You should only praise God that you can see," they said. "Jesus made mud on the Sabbath. He's a sinner, not a miracle worker."

"I don't know if he's a sinner," the man answered. "I do know that once I was blind. Now I see."

Find It in the Bible
JOHN 9:10–25

MUD ON A BLIND MAN'S EYES
PART THREE

I already told you, Jesus gave me my sight," said the once-blind beggar. "Do you want to be his follower like me?"

The Pharisees cursed him. "You follow Jesus. But we're followers of Moses. We know that God spoke to Moses. But we don't know where Jesus comes from."

"This is amazing!" exclaimed the man. "You don't know where he comes from? He opened my eyes! Everybody knows that God doesn't listen to sinners. God listens to those who worship and obey him. Since the world began, no one born blind could see. If Jesus weren't from God, he couldn't do this."

"You were born a sinner," said the Pharisees. "Do you think you can teach us?" They threw him out. "You can't be a Jew anymore."

Jesus heard they'd thrown the man out. Jesus went looking for him. He found the man and asked, "Do you believe in the Son of God?"

"Who is he, sir?"

"You've seen him. He's speaking with you right now," Jesus answered.

"Lord, I believe." And the man worshiped Jesus.

Find It in the Bible
JOHN 9:26–41

JESUS—THE GOOD SHEPHERD

A shepherd keeps his sheep safe in a barn. The shepherd always goes into the barn through the door. A thief sneaks into the barn another way. The shepherd knows his sheep by name, and they know his voice. They won't follow a stranger."

Jesus was explaining why the once-blind man followed him. But the people couldn't understand his meaning. So he tried again: "This is the truth. I'm the barn door. All who came before me are thieves. But the sheep didn't listen to them. Remember, I'm the door. Anyone who enters through me will be saved. They'll go in and out of the pasture. The thieves come to kill. I came that people would have life, overflowing life.

"I'm the good shepherd. The good shepherd gives his life for the sheep. I know my own sheep and my sheep know me. Just like the Father knows me and I know my Father."

"You're only human. God isn't your father!" Some of the Jews picked up stones to throw at Jesus.

"I've done many of my Father's good works. Is this why you want to stone me?" When they tried to arrest Jesus, he escaped.

Find It in the Bible
JOHN 10:1–39

DAY 265
LAMBS AMONG WOLVES

Jesus sent out seventy disciples, in pairs, to every town that he would soon visit. "There's a harvest of people out there," he told them. "Pray the Lord of the harvest for more laborers.

"I send you like lambs among wolves. Don't carry a backpack or money or extra shoes. When you go into someone's house, say, 'Peace to this house.' When people welcome you to town, eat the food they offer. Cure their sick. Tell them, 'The kingdom of God has come near you.' Whoever listens to you listens to me. If they turn you away, they've turned me away."

The seventy apostles returned full of joy. "Lord, in your name even the evil spirits obey us!"

"Don't rejoice over this," he said. "Instead, rejoice that your names are written in heaven."

Nearby stood a lawyer who knew the Jewish law. This man asked the Lord, "What should I do to get eternal life?"

"What does the law say?" asked Jesus.

"Love God with your whole heart," answered the lawyer. And love your neighbor like you love yourself."

"That's right. Do this and you'll have life," said Jesus.

Find It in the Bible
Luke 10:1–24

THE GOOD SAMARITAN

The lawyer wanted to trick Jesus. He asked, "Who is my neighbor?"

Jesus answered with a story: "A man traveled from Jerusalem to Jericho. He was robbed and beaten by bandits. As he lay on the road, a priest walked right by. So did a Levite. But a Samaritan had pity. He washed and bandaged the traveler's wounds and carried him to a nearby inn. This Samaritan paid the innkeeper to care for the man.

"Which of these three were the wounded man's neighbor?"

"The man who had pity."

"Right," said Jesus. "Go and do the same."

Find It in the Bible
LUKE 10:29–37

JESUS IS THE RESURRECTION
PART ONE

A man named Lazarus lay sick in Bethany, Mary and Martha's village. These women sent a message to Jesus: "Lazarus is sick." But when Jesus heard this, he waited two days. Then Jesus said to the disciples, "Let's go back to Judea."

"But, teacher," they said, "people want to kill you there."

"Our friend Lazarus has fallen asleep," he said. "I'm going to awaken him."

"Well, Lord, if he's only asleep he'll be fine." Jesus meant that Lazarus was dead. The disciples didn't understand this.

When Jesus got to Bethany, Lazarus had been dead four days. Martha went out to meet Jesus while Mary stayed home. "Lord, if you'd been here," she said, "Lazarus wouldn't have died. But I know God will give you anything you ask."

"Your brother will return from death."

"I know, Lord," said Martha. "He'll come back with the resurrection on the last day."

Find It in the Bible
JOHN 11:1–24

JESUS IS THE RESURRECTION
PART TWO

I am the resurrection and the life," said Jesus to Martha. "Those who believe in me may die, but they'll live again. Do you believe this, Martha?"

"Yes, Lord," Martha replied. "I believe you're Christ, God's Son, who has come into the world." Then she hurried home.

"Mary," whispered Martha, "the Teacher is here. He wants to see you." The Jews saw Mary leave and followed her. They thought she was going to Lazarus' tomb to weep. But they found her kneeling at Jesus' feet.

"Lord, you should have been here," Mary wept. "Then Lazarus wouldn't have died." Jesus saw her weeping. He looked up and saw all her Jewish friends weeping. This troubled him.

"Where did you bury him?"

"Come and see, Lord."

Jesus began to weep. "See how much he loved Lazarus?" some said.

But others said, "He made the blind man see. Couldn't he have kept this man from dying?" These words made Jesus sad.

Find It in the Bible
JOHN 11:25–37

JESUS IS THE RESURRECTION
PART THREE

L azarus' tomb was covered by a boulder. "Remove it," he said.

"Lord," complained Martha, "the body's begun to stink."

"Martha, I told you to believe and you'd see God's glory. Thank you, Father. You've heard me." Jesus said this so the people would believe in him. He spoke loudly: "Lazarus, come out."

Many Jews saw Lazarus come forth and believed. Others told the Pharisees who worried, "Soon everyone will believe in him." So they plotted to kill Jesus.

Find It in the Bible
JOHN 11:38–53

SET FREE ON THE SABBATH

The Lord was teaching at a synagogue on the Sabbath. Into the room walked a woman controlled by a crippling spirit. She'd been bent over for eighteen years. She had no way to stand up straight. Jesus saw her and called her over. "Woman," he said, "you're set free from your disability." He touched her with his hands. Instantly, she stood up straight and praised God.

But the leader of the synagogue was furious. Jesus had cured the woman on the Sabbath. It was against the law to work on the Sabbath. The leader spoke to the crowd: "There are six days in the week to work. Come on those days to be cured, not on the Sabbath."

The Lord answered him, "You faker. You all untie your donkey on the Sabbath. Then you lead it away to give it water. This woman is a daughter of Abraham. Satan has crippled her for eighteen long years. Shouldn't she be set free from this on the Sabbath?"

When he said this, all his enemies were put to shame. The entire crowd rejoiced to see the wonderful things he did.

Find It in the Bible
LUKE 13:10–17

GOD'S SEARCH FOR SINNERS
PART ONE

Tax collectors and sinners gathered to hear Jesus. Pharisees and other religious people grumbled: "Jesus welcomes sinners and even eats with them."

So Jesus told them this story: "Suppose you have a hundred sheep and lose one. Don't you leave the ninety-nine to search for the lost sheep? When you find it, you return with joy. You say to your friends, 'Rejoice with me! I've found my lost sheep.' So listen to me. There's great joy in heaven when one sinner turns away from sin. Much more than over ninety-nine law-keepers like you."

Find It in the Bible
LUKE 15:1–13

GOD'S SEARCH FOR SINNERS
PART TWO

Jesus thought this story would help them:
"A man had two sons. He divided his property between them. The younger son took his share and went to a faraway country. He spent everything he had there in foolish living. Then famine came to the land. With no food, he worked feeding pigs. He had to eat the pigs' food.

At last, he started thinking sensibly. "My father's servants have food. But here I am starving! I'm going home. I'll say, 'Father, I've sinned against heaven and against you. Don't call me your son anymore. Make me one of your hired workers.'"

"He set off for home. His father saw him coming. Filled with love, he ran and hugged his son. The young man said, 'Father, I've sinned against you. I shouldn't be called your son anymore.' But his father interrupted.

" 'Quickly,' the father told his servants, 'bring my best clothes for him. Put a ring on his finger and shoes on his feet. Let's eat and celebrate! My son was dead and now he's alive. He was lost and now he's found.' They began to celebrate."

Find It in the Bible
LUKE 15:11–24

GOD'S SEARCH FOR SINNERS
PART THREE

Y ou lawkeepers should know about the father's older son," Jesus continued.

"Hearing music, he asked what was happening. 'Your brother has come home safe and sound. So your father is giving a feast for him.'

"The older son was angry. So his father came out and asked him to come and celebrate.

" 'Listen,' the son answered, 'I've been working for you for years. I've worked like a slave and never disobeyed. But I've not even had a little party with my friends. Now this son of yours comes back. He's wasted your property in sin. And you throw a huge feast!'

" 'Son,' answered the father, 'you're always with me. Everything that's mine is yours. We must celebrate and rejoice. Your brother was dead and has come to life. He was lost and has been found.' "

Remember that the Pharisees had grumbled because Jesus ate with sinners. He told these stories so they would understand why he did this. Jesus hoped the lawkeepers would see why God loves sinners.

Find It in the Bible
LUKE 15:25–32

LAZARUS AND THE RICH MAN

Jesus told another story:

"A rich man had fine clothes and excellent food. Another man, Lazarus, was covered with sores and begged for scraps in the street. Dogs licked his sores.

"Lazarus died. Angels carried him to Abraham.

"The rich man died and was in torment. Far away, he saw Abraham with Lazarus at his side. He called, 'Father Abraham, have mercy. Send Lazarus with a drop of water to cool my tongue. I'm in agony in these flames.'

" 'Child,' answered Abraham, 'remember, in life you had good things. Lazarus had evil. Now he's comfortable and you're suffering. No one can come back.'

" 'Father,' said the rich man, 'Send Lazarus to warn my brothers. Then they won't have to suffer like me.'

" 'They should listen to the words of Moses and the prophets.'

" 'No, Father Abraham. If someone comes from the dead, then they'll listen.'

" 'They don't listen to Moses. If someone comes back from death, they won't listen to him, either.' "

Find It in the Bible
LUKE 16:19–31

THE HUMBLE AND THE HONORED

This story is to inspire people to always pray:

"There was a judge who didn't fear God or respect people. He refused to be fair to a widow. But she came back to him again and again. 'By law, you must be fair in this matter,' she said.

"Finally, the judge said, 'I don't respect anyone. But this widow's a bother. So I'll be fair in her case. Her demands will soon wear me out.'

"Pay attention to what this unfair judge said. Now, don't you think God will be fair when you pray? Will he wait? No. He'll act quickly. Yet when I return, will I find people praying in faith?"

Then he told another story. It's for people who think they're pure and look down on others:

"A Pharisee and a tax collector were praying. The Pharisee stood and prayed: 'Thank you I'm not like that tax collector. I always perform my religious duty.' Far away, the tax collector wouldn't even look up to heaven. In grief, he prayed: 'Have mercy on me. I'm a sinner.'

"Listen, God accepted him, not the Pharisee. Praise yourself and you'll be humbled. Humble yourself and you'll be honored."

Find It in the Bible
LUKE 18:1–14

"LET THE LITTLE CHILDREN COME"

Parents brought their children and tiny babies to Jesus. They only wanted him to touch them. But then the disciples noticed what these parents were doing. They sternly ordered them to stop.

But Jesus called for them. "Let the little children come to me. Don't stop them. The kingdom of God belongs to people like these children.

"I'll tell you the truth: You must receive the kingdom like a child. If not, you will never enter into it." Then he held the babies and gently touched the children.

Find It in the Bible
Luke 18:15–17

"YOUR FAITH HAS SAVED YOU"

Blind Bartimaeus sat by the Jericho road begging.

"Jesus is walking by," someone said.

"Jesus, Son of David," Bartimaeus shouted. "Have mercy on me!" The people in front sternly ordered him to be quiet. But Bartimaeus only shouted louder: "Son of David, have mercy on me!" Jesus stopped and ordered the man to be brought to him.

"What do you want me to do for you?"

"Lord, let me see again."

"Receive your sight," said Jesus. "Your faith has saved you." Instantly, Bartimaeus could see. He followed Jesus praising God with all the people.

Find It in the Bible
Luke 18:35–43

"SALVATION HAS COME
TO THIS HOUSE"

Bartimaeus and the crowd followed Jesus into Jericho. As he was passing through, more people gathered to see him. A man was there named Zacchaeus. He was a rich man because he was in charge of tax collecting. He was trying to see Jesus. But Zacchaeus was too short to see over the crowd. So he ran ahead to a sycamore tree. He climbed the tree to see over the people. Jesus was going to pass that way. Jesus came there, looked up, and said, "Zacchaeus, hurry down. I'm going to stay at your house today."

So Zacchaeus hurried down and happily welcomed Jesus to his house. But people grumbled, "Jesus is a guest in the house of a sinner."

Zacchaeus stood there in his house. "Lord," he said, "half of all I own I'll give to the poor. If I've cheated anyone, I'll pay them back four times as much."

"Today, salvation has come to this house." Jesus spoke to everyone within earshot. "Zacchaeus is a son of Abraham just as you are. Remember, the Son of Man came to seek out and save the lost."

Find It in the Bible
LUKE 19:1–10

DAY 279
"WHAT A WASTE!"

Jesus stayed in Bethany. A woman came with a little jar of expensive perfume. She poured it on Jesus' head as he sat at the table. The disciples were angry. "What a waste!" they said. "We could have sold it and given the money to the poor."

"Don't trouble her," Jesus said. "She's done a good thing. You always have poor people with you. I won't always be here. She's prepared my body for burial. Listen: The gospel will be preached all over the world. Then, what this woman has done for me will be remembered."

Find It in the Bible
MATTHEW 26:6–13

"YOUR KING IS HUMBLY COMING"

While Jesus was in Bethany, Judas, one of the disciples, went into Jerusalem. There he spoke with the leading priests: "What will you give if I betray Jesus to you?" They paid Judas thirty pieces of silver. From that moment, he looked for a chance to double cross the Lord.

Meanwhile, Jesus was headed for Jerusalem. "Go into the village ahead," he instructed two disciples. "You'll find a donkey and her colt that's never been ridden. Untie them and bring them to me. If anyone says anything to you, don't worry. Say, 'The Lord needs them.' He'll send them right away."

The two disciples found it just as he said. The owner asked them, "Why are you untying the donkey?" They said, "The Lord needs it." Then they brought him the donkey and her colt. They spread their cloaks over the animals' backs. Jesus rode the donkey from the Mount of Olives into Jerusalem.

Long before Jesus was born, Zechariah the prophet said this would happen. He wrote: "Look, Zion, your king is humbly coming to you. He's riding on a donkey and on a donkey's colt."

Find It in the Bible
MATTHEW 21:1–11; LUKE 19:28–35

DAY 281
"HOSANNA IN THE HIGHEST HEAVEN!"

Jesus rode down the Mount of Olives. People covered the path with their cloaks. Others spread palm leaves in the way. They praised God loudly and joyfully: "Blessed is the king who comes in the name of the Lord! Hosanna in the highest heaven!"

Some of the Pharisees said, "Teacher, order your disciples to stop."

He answered, "I tell you, if they were silent, the stones would shout."

Then Jesus saw Jerusalem and wept. "Your enemies will tear you down stone by stone," he said, "because you didn't notice the day God visited you."

Find It in the Bible
LUKE 19:36–44

THE HOUSE OF PRAYER

Jesus went into the temple in Jerusalem and drove out the people buying and selling and upset their money tables. People were there selling doves for sacrifices. Jesus knocked over their chairs. Then he announced: "This is written in the Scriptures: 'My house will be called a house of prayer; but you are making it a den of robbers.' "

The leading priests heard what he'd done. They kept looking for a way to kill Jesus. But they were afraid of him. The whole crowd was spellbound by his teaching.

The blind and disabled came to him in the temple. He cured them. The leading priests saw these amazing things. They heard the children joyfully shouting in the temple: "Hosanna to the Son of David!" This made the priests angry. "Do you hear what these children are saying?" they asked him.

"Yes," Jesus answered. "Haven't you ever read in the Scriptures: 'Praise has come from the mouths of infants and nursing babies'? You've prepared this praise for yourself?" Then he left for Bethany to spend the night.

Find It in the Bible
MATTHEW 21:12–17; MARK 11:15–19

THE STORY OF THE VINEYARD

Jesus told another story:

"A man planted a vineyard and built a winery there. He then rented the vineyard and went into another country. At harvest, the servants arrived to collect his share of fruit. But the renters beat one servant. They killed another and stoned a third. The man sent more servants, but they were treated the same. Finally, he sent his son. 'They'll respect my son,' the man thought.

" 'Here comes the owner's son,' said the renters. 'Someday this vineyard will be his. Let's kill him. Then the land will be ours.' So they tackled him and killed him.

"Answer this," continued Jesus. "When the owner comes, what will he do to those renters?"

"He'll put those villains to death," they answered. "He'll rent the vineyard to people who'll give him the fruit on time."

"Right," said Jesus. "So God's kingdom will be taken away from you. It will be given to people who produce the kingdom's fruit."

The leading priests heard his story. They knew Jesus was talking about them and wanted to arrest him. But they couldn't because the people saw Jesus as a prophet.

Find It in the Bible
MATTHEW 21:33–46

THE STORY OF THE WEDDING FEAST

Jesus told another story:

"A king gave a wedding feast for his son," he began. "He sent his servants to bring the invited guests. But they wouldn't come. So the king said, 'Tell them this: I've done everything. The wedding feast is ready; come and enjoy it.' But those he'd invited mocked the feast. They went away to their farms and businesses. Others hurt the king's servants and killed them.

"The king was enraged. His soldiers destroyed those murderers and burned their city. Then he told his servants, 'Go into the streets. Invite everyone to my son's wedding feast.' The servants invited the good and the bad people from the streets. The feast was filled with guests.

"The king came into the feast. He noticed a man who wasn't wearing wedding clothes. 'Friend,' he said, 'how did you get in without wedding clothes?' The man could say nothing. 'Tie him up,' commanded the king. 'Throw him out into the darkness. There people weep and grind their teeth with grief.' "

Jesus ended the story with this saying: "Many are called, but few are chosen."

Find It in the Bible
MATTHEW 22:1–14

WHAT TO GIVE TO GOD

The Pharisees were in charge of the Jewish religion. But the Romans ruled the land. Some Pharisees and Romans wanted to trick Jesus. "Teacher, we know you teach God's way. Tell us, should we pay taxes to the Roman emperor?"

"Why are you testing me?" asked Jesus. "You're phonies. Show me a coin that you'd use to pay taxes." They brought him a Roman coin. "Whose picture and title are on this coin?" Jesus asked.

"The emperor's picture," they answered.

"Right. So give the emperor what belongs to him. And give God what belongs to God." They heard this and were amazed. All they could do was leave him alone.

Later, Jesus taught his disciples more about giving to God. They were sitting near a room called the treasury. Here people brought gifts of money for the temple. Many rich people brought lots of money. A poor widow came with two pennies. Jesus said, "I'll tell you the truth. This widow has given more than all the others put together. They have plenty to give. She has nothing and has given everything she has."

Find It in the Bible
Matthew 22:15–22; Mark 12:41–44

THE STORY OF THE TEN BRIDESMAIDS

Jesus' disciples said, "Teacher, look at these beautiful temple buildings."

Jesus replied, "Not one of their stones will be left upon another. All this will be destroyed."

The disciples asked, "When will this happen, Lord?" Jesus answered them with this story:

"Ten bridesmaids had their lamps and were waiting to meet the bridegroom. Five of them were foolish. Five were wise. The foolish ones had lamps but no extra oil. The wise had extra oil for their lamps.

"At midnight, they heard a shout: 'The bridegroom is coming!' The bridesmaids lit their lamps. The foolish said to the wise, 'Give us some oil. Our lamps are going out.' But the others said, 'No, there's not enough for all of us. Go buy your own.'

"While they went to buy oil, the bridegroom arrived. He took the wise bridesmaids into the wedding feast. The door was shut. Then the other bridesmaids came. 'Lord, lord, open the door,' they called. The bridegroom answered, 'I don't know who you are.'"

"So be alert. You don't know the day or the hour when your Lord will come."

Find It in the Bible
MATTHEW 24:1,2; 25:1-13

JESUS TELLS OF HIS RETURN

When I come in glory, I'll sit on a glorious throne. All the nations on earth will gather there. I'll divide the people into two groups. This is like a shepherd who separates the sheep from the goats. I'll say to those on the right, 'Come here. You're blessed by my Father. Here's the kingdom he has waiting for you. I was hungry, and you gave me food. I was thirsty, and you gave me something to drink. When I was a stranger, you welcomed me. I was naked, and you gave me clothes. You visited me in prison.'

"Those people will ask, 'When did we do these things?'

" 'Here's the truth: You did this to the smallest member of my family. So you did it to me.'

"Then I'll speak to those on my left side. 'Get away from me. Go to the eternal fire that's ready for the devil and his angels. You never did any of these things for me. You did nothing for the littlest member of my family. So you never did it to me.' "

Then Jesus told his disciples: "The Passover is in two days. Then I'll be arrested and crucified."

Find It in the Bible
MATTHEW 25:31–46

THE LORD'S LAST MEAL

The Passover had come. Peter and John prepared the feast in a house in Jerusalem. Jesus and the disciples ate together in a large upstairs room. "I've been looking forward to this Passover," he said. "I want to eat this meal with you before I suffer. I'll never eat it again until the kingdom comes."

Jesus took a loaf of bread. "Take and eat this. It represents my body which is broken for you."

Then he took a cup of wine. "Take this and share it. It represents the blood which I will shed for forgiveness of sins."

Find It in the Bible
LUKE 22:7–20; MATTHEW 26:26–28

THE MASTER WASHES
HIS SERVANTS' FEET

Jesus got up from the meal and poured water into a pan. He brought a towel and began to wash his disciples' feet. It came to Peter's turn. He said, "Lord, are you going to wash my feet?"

Jesus answered, "You don't understand why I'm doing this. But later you'll see."

"You'll never wash my feet!" Peter declared.

"Unless I wash your feet, you don't belong to me. You call me 'Lord' and 'Master,' and I've washed your feet. So you should do the same to each other. The servants are not greater than their master."

Find It in the Bible
JOHN 13:3–16

DAY 290
"ONE OF YOU WILL BETRAY ME"

Jesus was troubled. "One of you will betray me," he said. The disciples looked at each other. They didn't know who he was talking about. Peter signaled John to ask Jesus who he was talking about.

"Lord," asked John, "who is it?"

"The one to whom I give this piece of bread." Jesus gave the bread to Judas Iscariot. Just then Satan entered into Judas. "Do what you're going to do quickly," Jesus said. No one at the table knew why he said this. Some thought that Jesus wanted Judas to buy something for the festival. Others thought it meant that Judas should give something to the poor. After he took the bread, Judas quickly went out. It was nighttime.

"I'll only be with you a little longer," said Jesus. "Here is a new commandment for you. Love one another just as I've loved you. You cannot come to the place I'm going. But you'll follow afterward."

Peter said, "Lord, why can't I follow you now? I'll lay down my life for you."

"I'll tell you what you'll really do. Listen for the rooster to crow tomorrow morning. By then, you'll have rejected me three times."

Find It in the Bible
JOHN 13:21–38

DAY 291
IN A GARDEN CALLED GETHSEMANE

They sang a hymn and went to the Mount of Olives. At a garden called Gethsemane, Jesus said, "Sit here. I'll go over there and pray." With Peter, James, and John, he went to pray. "I am deeply saddened," he told them. "Stay awake with me here." And Jesus went aside alone.

He threw himself on the ground praying, "My Father, don't make me do this. But this is what you want. So I'll give up what I want."

He found the three disciples sleeping. "Get up; let's go. It is time for me to be betrayed."

Find It in the Bible
MATTHEW 26:30–46

THE ARREST OF JESUS CHRIST

Judas Iscariot arrived at Gethsemane. With him was a large crowd with swords and clubs. They were sent by the leading priests. "The one I kiss is Jesus," Judas told them. "Arrest him."

Judas quickly walked to Jesus. "Hello, Teacher!" he said, and then he kissed him.

"Friend," said Jesus, "do what you came to do." Then he spoke to the crowd: "You've come to arrest me with swords and clubs. Am I a bandit? I taught you everyday in the temple. You didn't arrest me there." All the disciples ran from the garden, and Jesus was led away.

Find It in the Bible
MATTHEW 26:47–56

A ROOSTER CROWS; PETER WEEPS

They took Jesus into the high priest's house. Outside, the crowd waited. Peter joined them. A girl stared at him in the firelight. "He was with Jesus," she said.

"Woman," said Peter, "I don't know him."

Later, someone else said, "You're his follower."

"Man, I am not."

Then someone insisted, "He's from Galilee. I know this man was with Jesus."

"Man," Peter cursed, "I don't know what you're talking about!"

While Peter spoke, a rooster crowed. Jesus glanced at Peter. Jesus had mentioned that Peter would deny him. Peter remembered this, walked away, and bitterly wept.

Find It in the Bible
LUKE 22:54–62

DAY 294
"HE SHOULD DIE!"

That night, they mocked and beat and blindfolded Jesus. The next morning, the leaders and chief priests gathered. Guards brought Jesus to them. They said, "If you are the Christ, tell us."

He replied, "If I tell you, you won't believe. If I ask you questions, you won't answer. But from now on, I'll be seated at God's throne."

They asked, "Are you saying that you're the Son of God?"

"You say that I am," he answered.

"There!" they declared. "he said it himself. For this he should die!"

They tied Jesus up and led him away.

Find It in the Bible
LUKE 22:63–23:1

THE DEATH OF JUDAS ISCARIOT

Judas Iscariot, the man who betrayed Jesus, heard Jesus was to die. So he changed his mind about what he'd done. He brought the thirty pieces of silver back to the priests. "I've sinned," said Judas. "Jesus is an innocent man."

"Why should that matter to us?" answered the leading priests. "What you've done is your problem."

Judas threw the coins in front of the priests in the temple. Then he ran away and hanged himself. The priests took the silver. But they said, "Moses' law says we can't put this in the offering. It is money that was used for death." They talked about this problem for a while. Then they decided to buy the potter's field with the money. It would be used to bury people who weren't Jews. This is why this field has always been called the Field of Blood.

Hundreds of years before this happened, the prophet Zechariah predicted it would. "They took the thirty pieces of silver," wrote Zechariah. "This is the price set for the servant of Israel. They gave them as the price for the potter's field. This is as the Lord commanded."

Find It in the Bible
MATTHEW 27:3–10

"THIS MAN IS INNOCENT"

The priests and leaders went to Pilate's palace. Pontius Pilate was the Roman ruler in Jerusalem. Jesus stood in front of Pilate as they accused him: "This man says that he, not your emperor, is our king."

"Are you the Jews' king?" Pilate asked Jesus.

"You say I'm a king. But I came for one reason: To bring the truth."

"What is truth?" scoffed Pilate. Then he told the Jews, "This man is innocent."

But they insisted. "He upsets people everywhere, from Galilee to Jerusalem."

"Herod is in charge in Galilee," said Pilate. "Take him to Herod."

Find It in the Bible
LUKE 23:1–7; JOHN 18:28–38

"CRUCIFY HIM! CRUCIFY HIM!"

Herod was happy. He'd heard of Jesus and hoped he'd do a miracle for him. This was his chance. But Jesus didn't answer any of his questions. The leading priests kept up their complaints about Jesus. Herod and his soldiers treated him shamefully and mocked him. Finally, they sent him back to Pilate. Jesus arrived wearing a royal robe. This was a joke about Jesus being king.

"This man hasn't done anything wrong," Pilate told them. "Herod doesn't seem to think so either. That's why he sent Jesus back to me. He's done nothing worth dying for. I'll just whip him and let him go." By this time many people had gathered.

"Away with him!" shouted the crowd. "Let Barabbas out of prison instead." Barabbas was a murderer. But Pilate still wanted to let Jesus go. The crowd kept shouting, "Crucify him! Crucify him!" Pilate tried one more time, but they shouted him down. So Pilate let the murderer Barabbas out of prison. He then took Jesus, had him whipped, and gave him to the crowd.

Herod and Pilate had never liked each other. But the day they questioned Jesus, the two men became friends.

Find It in the Bible
LUKE 23:8–25

CRUCIFIED WITH CRIMINALS

They took Jesus away. The crowd made Simon of Cyrene carry Jesus' cross. Women mourned for Jesus. "Don't weep for me," he said. "Weep for yourselves. One day soon you'll cry to the mountains, 'Cover us! Our enemies have come to kill us!' "

Two criminals were led away to die with Jesus. At a place called the Skull, the men were nailed to crosses. Jesus was crucified with a criminal on each side. The soldiers played gambling games to win Jesus' clothes. The leaders scoffed at Jesus. "He saved others. If he's God's Christ, he should save himself." The soldiers also mocked him by offering vinegar to drink. Even Pilate put a sign on the cross: "THIS IS THE KING OF THE JEWS."

One of the crucified criminals joined the cursing. "Are you the Christ? Save yourself and us."

"Don't you fear God?" said the other. "We deserve to be crucified. But this man's done no wrong." Then he said, "Jesus, remember me when you come into your kingdom."

"I'll tell you the truth," answered Jesus, hanging from his cross. "Today you'll be with me in Paradise."

Find It in the Bible
LUKE 23:26–43

THE DEATH OF JESUS CHRIST

Darkness fell as Jesus hung on the cross. Darkness continued from noon to three that afternoon. Then Jesus loudly cried, "My God, my God, why have you abandoned me?" People watching thought he called Elijah. Then he said, "It is finished" and stopped breathing. At that moment, the curtain in the temple was torn. It ripped from top to bottom. This opened the holy of holies. An earthquake rumbled across the land, and the rocks were split.

The captain of the Roman guards saw these things and was terrified. "Absolutely, this man was God's Son," he declared.

Find It in the Bible
MATTHEW 27:45–54; JOHN 19:30

A NEW TOMB IN THE ROCK

That evening, Joseph from Arimathea took Jesus' body from the cross. Together with Nicodemus, he wrapped the body in spices and clean linen. They laid it in a new tomb Joseph had cut in the rock. A heavy rock was rolled across the tomb's door. They left the garden.

The leading priests and Pharisees went to Pilate. "That liar, Jesus, said he'd come back from death," they said. "Send soldiers to guard the tomb for three days. Then his disciples can't steal the body." So they sealed the tomb shut and set guards over it.

Find It in the Bible
MATTHEW 27:57–66; JOHN 19:38–42

DAY 301
"HE'S LEFT DEATH BEHIND"

The sun was rising Sunday morning, the third day since Jesus' death. Mary from Bethany and Mary Magdalene came to his tomb. Suddenly, an earthquake rumbled. An angel had rolled away the stone. He sat by the open tomb, flashing like lightning. The guards fell down, stunned with fear.

The angel spoke: "Don't be afraid, women. I know you're looking for Jesus. He isn't here. He's left death behind, just as he said he would. Here, look where he lay. Quickly, go tell his disciples this: Jesus is waiting for them in Galilee. Meet him there."

Find It in the Bible
MATTHEW 28:1–7

"I'VE SEEN THE LORD!"

Mary Magdalene stood alone, weeping by the tomb. She turned around. There was Jesus! But Mary thought he was the gardener. "Sir," she said, "have you taken away my Lord? Tell me where you've laid him."

Jesus said to her, "Mary."

"Teacher!"

"Don't hold onto me," he said. "I haven't yet gone up to my Father. Go and tell my brothers this: I'm going up to my Father and your Father. I'm going to my God and your God."

Mary Magdalene went and announced to the disciples, "I've seen the Lord!" She told them what had happened.

Find It in the Bible
JOHN 20:1–18

JESUS WALKS TO EMMAUS

That day, two disciples traveled from Jerusalem to Emmaus. They talked together about the things that had happened. A man began walking with them. They didn't recognize Jesus. "What are you talking about?" Jesus asked them.

"Haven't you heard about Jesus? He was a mighty prophet who was just crucified. But angels told some women he's now alive. Then his tomb was found empty."

"Don't you know that this had to happen to Christ?" Jesus explained the writings of Moses and the prophets to them. He showed them what the Scriptures said about Christ.

Find It in the Bible
LUKE 24:13–27

JESUS APPEARS IN JERUSALEM

PART ONE

The two disciples didn't recognize Jesus. In Emmaus, they sat down to eat together. Jesus took the bread, blessed it, and broke it. When he gave it to them, they saw who he was. But Jesus had vanished.

They rushed back to Jerusalem and told the disciples: "Our hearts were burning within when he spoke to us on the road."

And they were told: "Jesus has appeared to Peter, too!" Just then they were startled and terrified. Jesus himself stood among them.

"Peace be with you," he said. But they thought they were seeing a ghost.

Find It in the Bible
LUKE 24:28–37

JESUS APPEARS IN JERUSALEM

PART TWO

Returning from death, Jesus stood with his disciples in Jerusalem. "Why is there doubt and fear in your hearts? Touch me and see." The disciples were so happy but couldn't believe their eyes. "Have you anything to eat?" asked Jesus. They watched while Jesus ate.

As he opened their spiritual understanding, they heard what Moses and the prophets had written about him. "Christ will suffer and rise from the dead, and the whole world will know it," said Jesus. "You've seen and understood all this.

"Soon I'll send you the Holy Spirit as my Father promised. Stay here in the city until power from above covers you like clothing."

The disciple named Thomas didn't see these things. He didn't believe it had happened. "I'll have to touch his wounds before I believe," he said. A week later, the doors were shut. Suddenly, Jesus stood among them.

"Reach out, Thomas," he said. "Touch my hands. Don't doubt; believe."

"My Lord and my God," answered Thomas as he touched Jesus.

Find It in the Bible
LUKE 24:38–49; JOHN 20:24–28

JESUS SERVES BREAKFAST
ON THE SEASHORE

Seven of Jesus' disciples, including Peter, agreed to go fishing in the Sea of Tiberias. Fishing all night, they caught nothing.

At daybreak, Jesus stood on the beach. The disciples didn't know it was Jesus.

"Children," he called, "you have no fish, do you?"

"No," they replied.

"Cast your net on the right side of the boat. There you'll find some." So the disciples cast the net. They weren't able to haul it into the boat. It was full to bursting with fish.

John exclaimed to Peter, "It's the Lord!" When Peter heard this, he jumped overboard into the sea. The other disciples rowed ashore dragging the net full of fish. They weren't far from shore, so Peter swam to the beach. There they found a fire with fish and bread cooking on it.

"Bring some more fish," said Jesus. They dragged the net ashore. It was full of 153 big fish, but the net wasn't torn. "Come and have breakfast," invited Jesus.

Find It in the Bible
JOHN 21:1–12

DAY 307
"DO YOU LOVE ME?"

As they stood by the fire, no disciple dared ask, "Who are you?" They knew it was the Lord. Jesus took the bread and gave it to them. He did the same with the fish.

When they finished breakfast, Jesus spoke to Peter: "Peter, do you love me more than these fish?" "Yes, Lord. You know that I love you."

"Then feed my lambs," Jesus replied. Then he asked Peter the same question a second time. "Do you love me?"

"Yes, Lord. You know that I love you."

"Then tend my sheep." Then, for a third time, Jesus asked, "Do you love me?" Peter felt hurt that Jesus had to ask this so many times.

"Lord," he answered, "you know everything. You know that I love you."

Jesus said, "Feed my sheep. I'll tell you the truth, Peter. When you were young, you did whatever you wished. But when you're old it will be different. Someone else will take you where you don't want to go." This meant that Peter would someday die because he served God.

Jesus did so many things. The world can't hold all the books that could be written about him.

Find It in the Bible
JOHN 21:12–25

DAY 308
JESUS IS TAKEN INTO HEAVEN

Jesus Christ proved that he was alive many times. For forty days, he stayed with the disciples, speaking about God's kingdom. He ordered them not to leave Jerusalem. Rather, they were to wait there for the Father's promise. "I mentioned this to you before," he said. "John baptized with water. But in a few days, you'll be baptized with the Holy Spirit."

"Lord," they asked, "is now the time you'll bring the kingdom to Israel?" They were gathered together on the Mount of Olives.

"You can't know the times the Father has set for these things. But you will receive power. The Holy Spirit will come upon you like clothing. Then you'll speak for me starting in Jerusalem. Then in Judea, Samaria, and to the ends of the earth."

After Jesus said this, he was lifted up as they watched. Then a cloud took him out of sight. While he was going, the disciples gazed toward heaven. Two men wearing white clothes stood with them. "Men from Galilee, why are you standing there looking up? This Jesus has been taken from you into heaven. But he'll come back in the same way as you saw him go."

Find It in the Bible
ACTS 1:3–11

PENTECOST IN JERUSALEM
PART ONE

The disciples constantly prayed together after Jesus went away in the cloud.

Fifty days after Jesus was crucified, there was a big holiday. It was called Pentecost. At that time, many thousands of people visited Jerusalem. The disciples were all together that day. Suddenly, a sound like violent wind filled the house. Fire appeared and rested on each of them. They were all filled with the Holy Spirit. The Spirit made them able to speak in other languages. Then a curious crowd gathered. They were from many different nations. But they each heard the gospel in their own language.

Find It in the Bible
ACTS 2:1–11

PENTECOST IN JERUSALEM
PART TWO

Everyone was amazed and puzzled. They each heard their own language! "What does this mean?" some asked. Others sneered, "They're drunk on new wine."

Then Peter stood up. "People from Judea and all who live in Jerusalem, we're not drunk. It's only nine in the morning. Long ago, the prophet Joel wrote: 'In the last days I'll pour my Spirit on everyone. Then those who call on the Lord's name will be saved.'

"Jesus of Nazareth did miracles among you, but in God's plan, you killed him. This same Jesus God brought back from death. We have seen him. He's now at God's right hand. The Father has given Jesus the promise of the Holy Spirit."

Peter's words cut them to the heart. They asked, "What shall we do?"

"Everyone, turn from your sins, be forgiven, and be baptized in the name of Jesus Christ. You'll be given the Holy Spirit as a gift. This promise is for you, your children, and all who are far away." Three thousand people believed in Jesus that day.

Find It in the Bible
ACTS 2:12–41

DAY 311
WALKING AND LEAPING
AND PRAISING GOD

Give me money, please," begged a disabled man near the temple. "I've been crippled since I was born." Peter and John, passing nearby, heard the man's plea.

"I have no silver or gold," Peter said to him, "but I'll give you what I have. In the name of Jesus Christ of Nazareth, stand up and walk." Peter took the man's hand and helped him up. Instantly, the man's feet and ankles became strong. Jumping up, he walked. The man went into the temple with Peter and John. He was walking and leaping and praising God.

Find It in the Bible
Acts 3:1–8

ARRESTED IN THE TEMPLE

People of Israel," Peter spoke in the temple, "why are you amazed and wondering about this man? He wasn't healed because we are powerful or holy. This is the way your ancestor's God has glorified his Son, Jesus. Pilate wanted to free Jesus, but you wanted the murderer Barabbas instead. And so you killed the source of life. But God brought him back from death. We have seen him. Faith in the name of Jesus Christ has made this man strong.

"I know that you didn't know what you were doing. You ignorantly killed Jesus. The prophets all said this would happen to Christ. But now, turn to God so your sins will be wiped out. Then refreshing times will come because of the Lord. In time, God will send Jesus, your Christ, back again."

Peter and John were speaking to the people. The priests and the temple captain came to them. These men were annoyed that the disciples were teaching in the temple, especially that they said, "In Jesus, there is return from death." So they arrested Peter and John. They were held until the next day. But five thousand people believed in Jesus that day.

Find It in the Bible
Acts 3:9–4:4

THE COMPANIONS OF JESUS

The next day, Peter and John stood in front of the high priest and other leaders. "In whose name did you do this work?" they were asked.

Peter was filled with the Holy Spirit. "Leaders of the people," he said, "do you want to know why this man is standing here in good health? It is by the name of Jesus Christ of Nazareth—the man you crucified, and God brought back from death. Salvation is only found in him. No other name has been given by which we must be saved."

The leaders saw Peter and John's boldness. They saw that they were common, uneducated men. Also, they knew Peter and John were companions of Jesus. The priests and leaders were amazed.

"What should we do with them?" they asked each other. "Everyone in Jerusalem has heard of this miracle. We can't say it didn't happen." So they ordered the disciples, "Never speak again in the name of Jesus."

"We can't keep from speaking of what we've seen and heard," they answered. And the people praised God for what had happened.

Find It in the Bible
ACTS 4:5–21

"YOU LIED TO GOD!"

With great power and in one accord, the apostles declared the Lord's resurrection. Great grace was upon them all. Those who owned houses sold them. The money was given to those who were in need.

But a man named Ananias sold some property. His wife, Sapphira, agreed that they keep some of the money. Only part of it was given for the poor.

"Ananias," said Peter, "why has Satan caused you to lie? The Holy Spirit knows you held back part of the money. When you sold the land, the money was yours. Now, you have lied to God!"

Hearing this, Ananias fell down and died. Young men took the body out for burial. Later, Ananias's wife came in. She didn't know what had happened. "Did you and your husband sell your land?" asked Peter.

"Yes," Sapphira answered.

"Why did you test the Lord's Spirit? There are the men who buried your husband. They're ready to carry you out." Immediately, she fell to the floor, dead. Sapphira was buried beside her husband. And the fear of God came over the whole church.

Find It in the Bible
ACTS 4:32–5:11

ARRESTED IN THE TEMPLE AGAIN

Great numbers of men and women be-lieved. The sick were even carried out into the streets of Jerusalem. They simply wanted Peter's shadow to fall on them as he passed by. People brought the sick in from the towns around. They all were cured.

Then the high priest took action. He and the other priests and teachers were jealous. So they arrested the apostles and put them into prison. But during the night, an angel opened the prison doors. "Go," said the angel. "Stand in the temple and tell the people about this life." So at dawn, the apostles were in the temple again. There they went on with their teaching.

That day, the priests called for the prisoners to be brought. But the police didn't find the apostles in the prison. "We found the prison locked," they reported. "The guards were standing at the doors. But no one was inside." Everyone was puzzled.

Then another report came: "The men you put in prison are teaching in the temple!" The temple police quietly brought the apostles to the high priest. They were afraid of being stoned by the people.

Find It in the Bible
ACTS 5:14–26

FIGHTING AGAINST GOD

T he apostles stood in the council. "We gave you strict orders!" said the high priest. "Don't teach in this name again. Yet you've filled Jerusalem with your teaching."

Then Peter spoke for all the apostles: "We must obey God instead of any human power. You hanged Jesus on a cross and there he died. But God brought him back from death. Now Jesus is by God's side as the Leader and Savior. He wants to give Israel forgiveness of sins. We simply speak of what we've seen."

The council was enraged and wanted to kill the apostles. But a wise teacher named Gamaliel spoke up. "Fellow Israelites, think carefully about this matter. I say, let them alone. If their work is merely human, it will fail. But if it comes from God, you can't stop them. In fact, you may be found fighting against God." The council was won over by Gamaliel's reasoning.

The apostles were whipped and ordered not to speak in Jesus' name. They were released rejoicing: "We are worthy to suffer for his name!" And they didn't stop declaring and teaching, "Jesus is the Christ."

Find It in the Bible
ACTS 5:27–42

A MAN FULL OF FAITH

God's word kept on spreading in Jerusalem. The number of disciples grew larger. Even a great many priests came to faith in Christ.

Seven men were chosen from among the believers. They were full of the Holy Spirit and wisdom. Their job was to care for the sharing of food among the believers. One of these was Stephen, a man full of faith, grace, and power. He did great wonders and signs among the people. Some among the Jews rose up and argued with Stephen. But they couldn't stand against his wisdom and spirit. So they secretly paid people to accuse him: "We've heard Stephen say terrible things against Moses and God." The people, leaders, and teachers of Moses' law were all angry.

Stephen was forced to go in to the council of rulers. There people lied about him. "He says Jesus of Nazareth will destroy the temple," they said. "He wants to change the traditions that Moses gave us."

The high priest looked at Stephen. "Are these things true?" he asked. The whole council also looked deeply into Stephen's face. They saw that it was like the face of an angel.

Find It in the Bible
ACTS 6:1–15

DAY 318
STEPHEN IS STONED TO DEATH

Stephen gave the council a meaningful speech. Beginning from Abraham, he traced the history of the Jewish people. But the council became enraged. "Your ancestors persecuted every prophet," Stephen said. "These prophets predicted that Christ would come—and now you're his murderers." With a shout, they rushed him. "Look," Stephen said, "the heavens are opened. There's Jesus standing next to God." They covered their ears and dragged him from Jerusalem. There Stephen was stoned to death. "Lord Jesus, receive my spirit," he prayed. Then he knelt, saying, "Don't hold this sin against them." And Stephen died.

Find It in the Bible
ACTS 7:2–60

DAY 319
SAUL—THE PERSECUTOR OF JESUS

A young man named Saul approved of Stephen's death. Then Saul began to run the believers out of Jerusalem. He breathed threats and murder against the disciples. Dragged from their houses, believers were jailed.

Saul went to the high priest for permission to go to Damascus. He planned to arrest men and women who followed Jesus' way. When Saul came near Damascus, a light from heaven flashed around him. He fell to the ground. A voice said, "Saul, Saul, why do you persecute me?"

"Who are you, Lord?" asked Saul.

"I'm Jesus, the one you're harassing."

Find It in the Bible
ACTS 9:1–5

DAY 320
SAUL—THE BELIEVER IN JESUS

Saul lay on the ground, blinded by a light from heaven. Jesus himself spoke: "Get up and go into the city. There you'll be told what to do." The men traveling with Saul were standing speechless. They heard the voice but saw no one. They led Saul by the hand into Damascus. For three days, Saul was blind and ate nothing.

Then the Lord spoke to a disciple named Ananias. "A man from Tarsus named Saul has seen a vision. In it, you, Ananias, touch him so he can see again. Go and do this."

"Lord," Ananias said, "I've heard of this man. He's done so much evil to your saints in Jerusalem. He's come here to arrest people who call on your name."

"Go, Ananias. I've chosen Saul to bring my name to people of all nations. He'll bring my name to kings and the people of Israel. I will personally teach him how much he must suffer. This suffering will be for my name."

Ananias went. "Brother Saul," he said, "the Lord Jesus has sent me. Receive your sight. Be filled with the Holy Spirit." Instantly, Saul could see again. He was baptized, ate a meal, and got his strength back.

Find It in the Bible
ACTS 9:6–19

DAY 321
SAUL—THE PREACHER OF JESUS

Saul stayed for several days with the disciples in Damascus. Immediately, he went to the Jewish synagogues. "Jesus is the Son of God," he declared.

"Isn't this the man who made havoc in the church in Jerusalem?" After a while, some people plotted to kill Saul. But Saul found out. The gates were watched day and night. So the disciples brought him to a hole in the city's wall. They lowered Saul down in a basket, and he escaped.

Saul returned to Jerusalem. He tried to join the disciples there. But they were afraid. "He doesn't believe in Jesus," they said. But a disciple named Barnabas introduced Saul to the apostles. Barnabas told them how Saul had seen the Lord.

"The Lord spoke to him in Damascus," said Barnabas. "And Saul boldly preached the gospel there." So Saul stayed with the church in Jerusalem. He spoke and argued with the Greek Jews, but they plotted to kill him. So the believers put Saul on a boat in Caesarea. From there, he sailed home to Tarsus.

And the whole church had peace and was built up.

Find It in the Bible
ACTS 9:19–31

"TABITHA IS ALIVE!"

Peter went here and there among all the believers. In Joppa was a disciple named Tabitha. She was faithful to do good works and help others. But she grew sick and died. Two men were sent to Peter. "Please come with us quickly," they said.

At Tabitha's house, the widows were weeping. Peter sent them out, knelt down, and prayed. Then he said, "Tabitha, get up." She opened her eyes and sat up. The news went out: "Tabitha is alive!" Many believed in the Lord.

Peter stayed in Joppa for some time in Simon the tanner's house.

Find It in the Bible
Acts 9:36–43

PETER'S VISION IN JOPPA

In Caesarea lived a Roman soldier named Cornelius. So Cornelius wasn't a Jew. He was a Gentile. Yet he was true to God and gave to the poor. He always prayed. One afternoon, this man had a vision. An angel came and said, "Cornelius?"

"What is it, Lord?" Cornelius stared at the angel in terror.

"Send men to Joppa and find Peter at Simon's house." Quickly, Cornelius sent for Peter.

About noon the next day, Peter went to Simon's roof to pray. While he waited, Peter fell into a trance. He saw a large sheet coming from heaven. In it were all kinds of animals. A voice spoke: "Peter, get up and eat these animals." But the animals in the sheet were banned by Jewish law. So, to Peter, the meat wasn't clean.

"No, Lord," said Peter. "I've never eaten any unclean meat."

"God has made this meat clean. Don't call it unclean again." Peter was puzzled about this. Just then the men came from Cornelius. The next day, Peter went with them to Cornelius's house in Caesarea.

Find It in the Bible
Acts 10:1–23

DAY 324
THE SPIRIT AND THE GENTILES

Cornelius's relatives and close friends were all gathered. Finally, Peter arrived. Cornelius fell at Peter's feet to worship him. "Get up," said Peter. "I'm only a mortal man."

In the house, Peter said, "You know that I'm a Jew. It's against our law to visit a Gentile. But God told me not to call anyone unclean." This was the meaning of Peter's vision two days before. "So I had no problem coming here. What do you want?"

Cornelius replied, "Four days ago, a man in dazzling clothes came to me. 'Cornelius,' he said, 'God has heard your prayers. Send to Joppa and find Peter.' I did this, and you're kind enough to come. We're here in the presence of God to listen to you."

So Peter began to tell them the good news about Jesus Christ. He mentioned forgiveness of sins in Jesus' name but had to stop. The Holy Spirit had fallen on everyone listening. The Jewish believers with Peter were astounded. The Father's gift of the Holy Spirit had been poured on the Gentiles! "Let's baptize these people in the name of Jesus Christ," said Peter. And they stayed there for several days.

Find It in the Bible
ACTS 10:24–48

THE LORD RESCUES PETER

King Herod laid his violent hands on some of the believers. He had James, John's brother, killed. Then Peter was arrested. The church urgently prayed to God.

Peter slept chained to two soldiers. An angel entered the prison. "Get up, quickly. Put on your sandals." Peter did so. "Follow me." The apostle thought he was seeing a vision. They passed through the guards. By itself, the prison gate swung open. They walked along a city lane. The angel suddenly disappeared.

"The Lord has rescued me," realized Peter. "The people will not see me die."

Find It in the Bible
ACTS 12:1–11

PETER AND THE PRAYER MEETING

Peter realized he was saved from death. At once, he went to Mary's house, where the church was praying. Mary was Mark's mother.

Rhoda, Mary's maid, heard a knock on the gate. When she answered, Rhoda recognized Peter's voice. She was overjoyed. Instead of opening the gate, she ran to tell the others. "You're out of your mind," they said. But Rhoda insisted. They then said, "It's Peter's angel."

Meanwhile, Peter continued knocking. They opened the gate and were amazed. "Quiet, quiet," Peter whispered. He described what had happened to him. "Tell this to the Lord's brother, James, and to the believers," he said. Peter then went to another place.

In those days, Herod feuded with the people of Tyre. They came to him to make peace. They had no choice since King Herod controlled their food. Herod put on his royal robes and sat on his throne. He gave a vain speech to the people. "It's the voice of a god," they shouted. "Herod is more than a man!"

Instantly, an angel of God struck Herod down. He hadn't given God the glory. Herod, eaten up inside by worms, died.

Find It in the Bible
ACTS 12:12–23

THE BELIEVERS ARE CALLED CHRISTIANS

When Stephen was killed, believers scattered all over the Middle East. In Antioch, some told the Greeks the good news of Jesus. A great number of Gentiles became believers and turned to the Lord.

The church in Jerusalem heard of this. They sent Barnabas to Antioch. There he saw God's grace among the people. Barnabas rejoiced. "Be faithful to the Lord," he told them. "Stay devoted to him." Barnabas was a good man, full of the Holy Spirit and faith. A great many people were brought to the Lord.

Then Barnabas went to Tarsus to look for Saul. He found him and brought him back to Antioch. For an entire year, they met with the church. Barnabas and Saul taught many, many people. The believers there were not at all like Jews. And they'd changed in ways that made them unlike Gentiles. So it was in Antioch that believers were first called "Christians."

At that time, a famine came. Believers in Judea suffered without food. So the church in Antioch sent Barnabas and Saul. They brought aid to the churches in Judea.

Find It in the Bible
Acts 11:19–30

THE APOSTLES ARE SENT OUT

Now in the church at Antioch there were prophets and teachers. They prayed together worshiping God. The Holy Spirit said to them, "Set aside Barnabas and Saul. I've called them for my work." The leaders of the church prayed and laid their hands on them. The Holy Spirit sent Barnabas and Saul out. They took Mark and set off. The three apostles sailed to the island of Cyprus. There they spoke God's word in the Jewish synagogues.

They traveled through the whole island. At Paphos lived a magician, a false prophet named Bar-Jesus. The ruler of Cyprus, Sergius Paulus, wanted to hear God's word. But the magician tried to turn him away from the faith. Saul, now called Paul, watched him carefully. Paul was filled with the Holy Spirit. "You son of the devil," he said, "you enemy of all that's right, stop making the Lord's straight paths crooked. God's hand is against you. You'll not be able to see for a while."

Shortly, the magician could only see darkness. He had to have someone lead him by the hand. Sergius Paulus saw this and believed. He was delighted at the teaching about the Lord.

Find It in the Bible
ACTS 13:1–12

DAY 329
A LIGHT FOR THE GENTILES

Paul and his companions sailed away from Paphos. They reached the mainland at Pamphilia. There, Mark left them and returned to Jerusalem. The apostles traveled inland to another city named Antioch. This was in Pisidia. On the Sabbath, Paul spoke to the Jews in their synagogue. He traced the history of the Jewish people. This history ended with the death of Jesus. Paul told his listeners that Jesus had returned from death.

Almost the whole city gathered the next Sabbath. The Jews saw the crowds and became jealous. They denied that Paul spoke the truth. But Paul and Barnabas were bold. "God wanted his word to come to you first. But you don't seem to think you're worthy of eternal life. So we're going to tell the Gentiles. God has commanded this. He said, 'You're to be a light for the Gentiles. Then you can bring my salvation to the ends of the earth.' "

When the Gentiles heard this, they were glad. They praised the word of the Lord. The Lord's word spread all over the area. But the Jews drove Paul and Barnabas away. So they left, glad to shake Antioch's dust from their feet.

Find It in the Bible
ACTS 13:13–52

"THE GODS HAVE COME TO US!"

Paul and Barnabas were almost stoned like Stephen in Antioch. But they escaped to Lystra in Lycaonia.

Looking at a crippled man, Paul exclaimed, "Stand up on your feet!" And the man jumped up and began to walk. The crowds saw this.

"The gods have come down to us as men!" they exclaimed. "This one," they shouted, pointing at Barnabas, "is Zeus. The other man does all the talking. That means he's Hermes!" This was Paul. The priest of the temple of Zeus brought oxen for sacrifices.

Paul and Barnabas rushed into the crowd. "Friends!" they shouted. "Why are you doing this? We're human just like you. We've brought good news: Turn from these worthless things! The living God made heaven and earth and everything in them. He fills your bellies with food and your hearts with joy!" They were barely able to stop the sacrifices.

Then people came from Antioch and excited the crowd against Paul. He was stoned and dragged alive out of Lystra. Soon, the apostles returned to the church at Antioch in Syria.

Find It in the Bible
ACTS 14:1–26

"WE'RE SAVED THROUGH GRACE"

The Antioch church rejoiced. God had opened the door of faith for the Gentiles!

But then some people came to Antioch from Judea. They said, "You Gentile Christians must keep Moses' law."

But Paul and Barnabus said, "God is happy that the Gentiles have believed in Jesus. They don't have to do anything else to be saved." So the apostles and leaders called a meeting in Jerusalem. Paul and Barnabas went there to discuss this important problem.

The first person to speak was Peter. "Brothers, God gave the Gentiles the Holy Spirit. I was at Cornelius's house when it happened. So God must not see a difference between them and us. Anyway, no one has ever been able to keep Moses' law. We're saved through the grace of the Lord Jesus. So are the Gentiles."

Paul and Barnabas then told of the wonders God did among the Gentiles. James had the final word: "God wants to make the Gentiles into a people for his name. Let's not trouble those who are turning to God."

Find It in the Bible
ACTS 14:27–15:21

ACROSS THE SEA TO EUROPE

Then, Paul and Silas visited the places Paul had been before and strengthened the churches. The believers learned about the decision made in Jerusalem: They didn't have to keep the Jewish law. In Lystra, Paul met Timothy. This young disciple began to travel with Paul.

They traveled due west through Asia. The Holy Spirit didn't let Paul speak God's word there. At the coast of the Aegean Sea, the travelers stopped. This was the city of Troas. Here Paul met Luke, whom he called "the beloved physician."

That night, Paul had a vision of a man from Macedonia. Macedonia was a country across the Aegean Sea. The man begged, "Come help us!" Paul knew what this meant. God wanted him to leave Asia and cross the sea to Europe. There he would preach the good news.

Timothy, Luke, Silas, and Paul set sail. Two days later, they landed in Philippi, the main city in Macedonia. On the Sabbath, they went to the riverside. Speaking to the women who prayed there, they met Lydia. Her business was selling purple cloth. Soon, Lydia and her household were baptized. The apostles stayed in Lydia's house.

Find It in the Bible
Acts 16:1–15

PAUL AND THE FORTUNE-TELLER

L uke recorded the history of Paul's travels. He wrote the following story:

"In Philippi we met a slave girl who was controlled by a spirit. This spirit made her a fortune-teller. The girl's owners made money from her fortune-telling. She followed Paul around crying, 'These men serve the Most High God.' She did this for many days. Finally, Paul was annoyed. He spoke to the spirit. 'I order you in the name of Jesus Christ. Come out of her.' And it did.

"The slave girl's owners couldn't make money any longer from her fortune-telling. Angry, they forced Paul and Silas to the rulers at the marketplace. 'These men are disturbing our city,' they said. 'They want us to break the Roman law.' Paul and Silas were beaten and locked in the deepest prison cell.

"At midnight, Paul and Silas were praying and singing hymns. Other prisoners listened to them. Suddenly, a violent earthquake shook the prison. The doors opened, and the prisoners' chains fell off. The jailer awoke, saw the prison open, and grabbed his sword. He was about to kill himself. He thought his prisoners had escaped. But Paul shouted, 'Don't hurt yourself! We're all here.' "

Find It in the Bible
ACTS 16:16–28

PAUL, SILAS, AND THE JAILER

L uke's story continues:
"The jailer rushed into the prison. He fell down trembling in front of Paul and Silas. 'What do I have to do to be saved?'

" 'Believe in the Lord Jesus and you'll be saved with your household.' They spoke the Lord's word to him and his family. Next the jailer washed their wounds. Then he and his family were baptized. They sat down to a meal together rejoicing. The jailer had become a believer in God!

"Returning to Lydia's home, they encouraged the brothers and sisters. Then we left Philippi."

Find It in the Bible
ACTS 16:29–40

HARASSED BY JEALOUSY

In Thessalonica, Paul went into the synagogue to discuss the Scriptures. For three Sabbaths, he explained why Christ had to die. He proved that Christ had to come back from death. "The Christ is Jesus," said Paul. "He's the man I'm telling you about."

Some Jews, many Greeks, and important women joined Paul and Silas. Certain Jews formed a mob with ruffians from the marketplace. The city was in an uproar. People shouted, "These people have been turning the world upside down. Now they've come to our city!"

At the nearby town of Berea, Paul entered the synagogue. These Jews were more civil than those in Thessalonica. They welcomed Paul's message eagerly. "Are these things true?" they wondered. So they studied the Scriptures everyday. Many of them believed, as did some Greek women and noblemen.

But people from Thessalonica arrived. Crowds were stirred up, and Paul had to flee to the coast. Timothy and Silas stayed behind while Paul traveled to Athens. There he waited for his companions.

Find It in the Bible
ACTS 17:1–15

THE BABBLER SPEAKS OF GOD

Paul became known in Athens as a babbler. He constantly talked about Jesus Christ. Some people there did nothing but talk about new ideas. "We'd like to know what these strange notions mean," they told Paul.

"I found an interesting altar in your city," he began. "On it was written: To AN UNKNOWN GOD. I declare this God, who made the world and everything in it, to be the Lord of heaven and earth. He has no need of these shrines or anything humans can give. Instead, he gives us life and breath and all things."

Find It in the Bible
ACTS 17:16–25

DAY 337
ATOP A HILL IN ATHENS

Atop a hill in Athens, Paul declared the true God: "From one ancestor God made all the different races. He decided when and where on earth they would live. Why? So they would search for the Lord, reach out, and find him. He is not far from each of us. For in him we live and move and have our being. Your poets have said this very thing. They wrote: 'For we, too, are his children.' "

Paul continued, "Since we're God's children, how can God be a stone image shaped by human imagination? Now he commands all people to change their minds. A day has been set when the world will be judged. God has selected a man to be the judge. He's brought him back from death."

Paul's audience interrupted and scoffed. "A man brought back from death?" They laughed. But some joined Paul and believed.

After this, Paul left Athens and went to Corinth. There he worked with Aquila and his wife, Priscilla. They were tentmakers, as was Paul. Every Sabbath he would try to convince Jews and Greeks about Jesus.

Find It in the Bible
ACTS 17:26–18:4

PAUL WORKS LIKE A FARMER

When Silas and Timothy arrived in Corinth, Paul was very busy. He was always talking about the Scriptures with the Jews. He assured them that Jesus was the Christ. They argued and snubbed him. Paul shook the dust out of his cloak into their faces. "This means I'm through with you. You must answer to God for refusing the truth. I'm not to blame. Now I'm going to pay attention to the Gentiles."

One night, the Lord spoke to Paul in a vision. "Don't be afraid," he said. "Speak and don't be silent. I'm with you, and no one will harm you. Many people in Corinth belong to me."

Paul worked like a farmer among the people of Corinth. He planted the seeds of God's gospel for eighteen months. During that time, Paul wrote two letters to the believers in Thessalonica. He wanted them to live a holy, hardworking life. "Look forward to the day Jesus comes again," he wrote.

Priscilla, Aquila, and Paul then sailed for Syria. Priscilla and her husband stayed in a big city there called Ephesus. Paul continued his journey. After visiting Jerusalem, he arrived at Antioch and stayed there some time.

Find It in the Bible
ACTS 18:5–23

EVERYONE HEARD THE LORD'S WORD

Soon Paul set off on his third long journey. From Antioch, he traveled by land through his hometown of Tarsus. In time, he arrived back in Ephesus. For three months, Paul argued in the synagogue about God's kingdom. Finally, some people said evil things about God's way. So Paul and the believers began to meet in Tyrannus's auditorium. This went on for two years. Everyone living in Asia heard the Lord's word. The Jews heard the truth and so did the Greeks.

God did amazing miracles through Paul. If someone who was sick touched his handkerchief, they were healed. At that time, there were people who pretended to heal the sick. So they tried to use the name of the Lord Jesus. Sceva's seven sons once spoke to an evil spirit. "I command you by the Jesus that Paul preaches," they declared.

"I know Jesus," said the spirit. "I know Paul, too. But who are you?" And the man with the evil spirit leaped on them. He beat them badly. The seven men ran from the house naked and bleeding. Everyone in Ephesus heard of this. They were awestruck, and the name of Jesus was praised.

Find It in the Bible
ACTS 19:1–17

DAY 340
CONFUSION IN EPHESUS
PART ONE

Some magicians in Ephesus became believers and burned their magic books in public. So the Lord's word grew mightily and remained.

Then a huge commotion broke out. The temple of an idol named Diana was big business in Ephesus. A silversmith named Demetrius made and sold little shrines for this goddess. He called together all the workers in his trade. "We get all our money from this business," he said. "But Paul says that handmade gods aren't gods! Large groups of people have believed him. Our business may be ruined. Also, the temple of the great goddess Diana will be scorned. Her majesty, the praise of all Asia, will be destroyed."

This news enraged the silversmiths. "Great is Diana of the Ephesians!" they shouted. The city was filled with confusion. Everyone rushed together to the city's theater. Gaius and Aristarchus, Paul's friends, were dragged with them. Paul wanted to go into the crowd. Of course, his disciples wouldn't let him do this. Some of Asia's rulers were Paul's friends. They warned, "Don't go into the theater!"

Find It in the Bible
ACTS 19:18–31

CONFUSION IN EPHESUS
PART TWO

The outdoor theater in Ephesus filled up with noisy people shouting various things. A man named Alexander finally quieted the crowd. But when they found out he was a Jew, they shouted him down. "He doesn't worship Diana!" For two hours everyone shouted, "Great is Diana of the Ephesians!"

Then the town clerk got control. "Citizens of Ephesus!" he shouted. "Everyone knows that Ephesus keeps the temple of Diana. Her statue, which fell down to us from heaven, is here. No one can say this isn't true. So you should be quiet. Don't become violent. These men haven't robbed the temple. Nor have they cursed the goddess. Demetrius, you and the silversmiths should go to court. Take your problems there to be solved. There is no reason for this! The Romans are about to accuse the whole city of rioting. So everyone go home." And that was the end of it.

After the uproar was over, Paul gathered the Ephesian believers. He'd been there three years. After encouraging them, he said farewell and left for Macedonia.

Find It in the Bible
ACTS 19:32–20:1

PAUL TALKED; EUTYCHUS SLEPT

Paul cared for the believers in Macedonia. Then he stayed three months in Greece. Setting sail for Syria, he learned of a plot against his life. So he traveled by land back through Macedonia. After several months, Paul and his companions arrived in Troas.

On Sunday, they met to break bread. Since Paul was leaving the next day, he talked on until midnight. Many lamps lit the upstairs meeting room.

As Paul talked still longer, a young man named Eutychus slept. He was sitting in an open window. Suddenly, Eutychus crashed to the ground three floors below. Someone picked him up dead. Paul went down, picked him up, and said, "Don't weep. His life is still in him."

Then Paul went upstairs. He broke bread, ate, and continued to talk. This went on until dawn. Meanwhile, they took Eutychus away alive. Everyone was very comforted.

Paul then sailed down the coast of Asia. "Let's be in Jerusalem by Pentecost," he said. While in the port of Miletus, Paul sent a message to Ephesus. Soon the Ephesian elders were hurrying to meet with the apostle.

Find It in the Bible
ACTS 20:6-17

PAUL'S FAREWELL

The leaders of the church in Ephesus came to Miletus. "You know how I live my life," Paul began. "I humbly serve the Lord with tears. I suffer the plots against my life. If there's any way to help, I do it. I brought God's message to your city and your houses. I told everyone about turning to God and faith in Jesus.

"And now the Spirit is leading me to Jerusalem. Prison and hardship are waiting for me there. But I don't prize my life for my own sake. I just want to finish my work. This is the important thing: to declare the good news of God's grace.

"Now, I know that none of you will ever see my face again. I wasn't afraid to tell you God's whole purpose. So the rest is up to you. I hand you over to God and the message of his grace.

"Remember that I never asked for money. Instead, I worked with these two hands for myself and my friends. Remember the Lord's words: 'It's more blessed to give than to receive.' " They knelt together in prayer. The men from Ephesus wept. They'd never see Paul again.

Find It in the Bible
Acts 20:18–38

ON THE WAY TO JERUSALEM

The apostles sailed across the eastern end of the Great Sea. Luke continues the story:

"We landed at Tyre and found the believers. Through the Spirit they told Paul, 'Don't go on to Jerusalem.' After seven days, we were ready to leave. Everyone followed us out of the city. We knelt on the beach, prayed, and said farewell. Then we went on board the ship and they went home.

"A short voyage took us to Ptolemais and then to Caesarea. There we stayed with Philip. He had served with the martyr Stephen in Jerusalem. While we were there, a man named Agabus came down from Judea. Agabus warned us in this way: Taking Paul's belt, he tied himself up. 'These are the Holy Spirit's words,' he said. 'The Jews in Jerusalem will tie up the owner of this belt. They will give him to the Gentiles.' Then everyone urged Paul not to go to Jerusalem.

" 'What are you doing?' asked Paul. 'Your weeping is breaking my heart. I'm ready to die in Jerusalem for the Lord's name.'

"We said nothing more except: 'Let the Lord do what he wants.' "

Find It in the Bible
ACTS 21:1–14

DAY 345
PAUL ENTERS THE TEMPLE

Luke continues:

"We were warmly welcomed in Jerusalem. Paul visited James and the elders. He told them of God's work with the Gentiles. They praised God for this. Then James said, 'Paul, there are thousands of Jewish believers here. They all love Moses' law. But they think you teach Jews to throw out the law.' This wasn't true. Paul only taught all people to trust God's grace.

" 'These people will soon know you're here,' James continued. 'So please do this: Four men are going to take a vow in the temple. Go with them and pay their fees. Then everyone will know that you care for Moses' law.' Paul knew the Jews could keep the law if they wanted to. And the Gentiles didn't need to keep the law. Either way, God wants people to believe in Jesus. James and the elders in Jerusalem knew this, too.

"So Paul and the men entered the temple. Paul didn't do this to please God. He just wanted people to stop lying about him. But there in the temple were men who had harassed Paul in Asia. They spied their old enemy. 'Here's our chance to get Paul,' they plotted."

Find It in the Bible
ACTS 21:15-27

PAUL IS DRAGGED OUT OF THE TEMPLE

Everything went well for Paul in the temple. At least, until the men from Asia found him. "Israelites, help!" they cried, grabbing Paul. "This is the man who is against Moses' law and this temple. Look! He's brought Gentiles here and made this holy place filthy!" The people rushed together and dragged Paul out of the temple.

Paul was about to be killed, but Roman soldiers rescued him. Then the captain arrested Paul and chained him. "Who's this man?" asked the captain. "What's he done?" Some in the crowd shouted one thing. Some shouted another. There was such an uproar that he couldn't hear. Paul had to be carried off by the soldiers. "Away with him!" shouted the crowd.

At a safe distance from the crowd, Paul spoke to the captain. "I'm a Jew, a citizen of Tarsus. That's an important Roman city. Please let me speak to the people." The captain gave his permission.

Paul stood on the steps and signaled the crowd for silence. "Brothers and fathers," he began, "listen to what I have to say."

Find It in the Bible
ACTS 21:27–22:1

A SPEECH IN THE STREETS

The angry crowd heard their own language and stopped to listen. "I'm a Jew, born in Tarsus," Paul said. "But here in Jerusalem, I learned our ancestors' law. When the time came, I fought against the Christians. The high priest and elders can tell you this.

"They sent me to Damascus to arrest Christians there. On the way, about noon, a great light from heaven flashed. I fell to the ground. A voice said, 'Saul, Saul, why are you fighting me?'

" 'Who are you, Lord?' I asked.

" 'I'm Jesus of Nazareth.'

"In the city, a good Jewish man named Ananias met me. 'God has chosen you,' he said. 'You'll tell the world of what you've seen and heard. Now get up and be baptized, calling on his name.'

"I came back here and was praying in the temple. The Lord appeared. 'Get out of this city,' he said. 'The people won't listen to you.'

" 'But Lord, I agreed when they killed Stephen,' I reasoned.

" 'Go; I am sending you far away to the Gentiles.' "

When they heard the word "Gentiles," the crowd erupted with violent anger.

Find It in the Bible
Acts 22:2–22

SAVED FROM THE RAGING CROWD

Away with such a fellow from the earth!" the crowd raged. "He shouldn't be allowed to live." They shouted, threw off their cloaks, and tossed dust into the air. The captain hurried Paul into the building. They were about to whip him. Paul said, "This is against Roman law. I'm a citizen and have done no wrong."

The soldiers were afraid. They'd chained a Roman citizen and could be arrested for this. The captain didn't even know what Paul had done. So he brought the apostle to the priests and the Jewish council.

Find It in the Bible
ACTS 22:22–30

SAVED FROM THE JEWISH COUNCIL

Paul addressed the council. "Brothers," he began. "I've always lived for God."

The high priest interrupted. "Hit him in the mouth!" he ordered.

"God will hit you, you whitewashed wall!" Paul came back. "You pretend to judge me by the law. But hitting me breaks the law."

"Do you dare put down God's high priest?" someone asked.

"I didn't know he was the high priest," Paul replied. "The Scriptures say, 'Don't speak evil of your leaders.' "

Paul explained the truth about the resurrection. "Brothers," he declared, "I'm on trial because of one thing: The hope of the resurrection of the dead." So a great hubbub began. Some wanted to let Paul go. Others refused. The argument became violent.

The Roman captain thought, "They're going to tear Paul to pieces." So the soldiers went down and took him out by force.

That night, the Lord stood near Paul. "Be brave," he said. "You've spoken for me here. You'll speak for me in Rome, too."

Find It in the Bible
ACTS 23:1–11

PAUL AND 470 SOLDIERS

The next morning, more than forty people plotted against Paul. "We swear not to eat until we kill him," they agreed. They went to the council and told them their plans. "Call for Paul to come back for another meeting. We'll kill him before he gets here."

Meanwhile, Paul's nephew heard about this trap. He went to Paul and told him of the danger. "Take this young man to the captain," Paul said. "He has something important to tell him." Paul's nephew secretly told the captain about the planned ambush.

Then the captain gave these orders: "Get ready to leave by nine o'clock tonight. Take Paul to Caesarea. Call together two hundred soldiers, seventy horsemen, and two hundred spearmen. Provide a horse for Paul, and bring him to Felix, the governor." A letter was written to Felix explaining the matter. Paul's accusers were told, "Go to the governor with your problem."

That night, Paul and 470 Roman soldiers left Jerusalem. At Caesarea, they delivered the letter and the prisoner to the governor. "I'll hear your case. But not until your accusers get here." Paul was kept under guard in Herod's palace.

Find It in the Bible
Acts 23:12–35

PAUL SPEAKS TO FELIX
PART ONE

Five days later, the high priest Ananias came down to Caesarea. Some elders and a lawyer came along. Paul entered the governor's court, and the lawyer began to accuse him: "Your Excellency, thank you for the peace and favor you've given us. I'll keep this short. This man is a pest in our nation. He stirs up Jews all over the world. He's a leader of a sect called the Nazarenes. He even tried to infect the temple with Gentiles. We wanted to judge him ourselves. But the captain took him away from us. That's why we're here today." Ananias joined in accusing Paul. He agreed with all the lawyer said.

Paul then spoke to Felix. "I'm happy to tell you my side of this story," he began. "I went to worship in Jerusalem twelve days ago. I didn't argue with anyone or stir up the crowds. They can't prove the things they say against me. I worship my ancestors' God, believing the law and the prophets. My hope in God is the same as theirs. I always do my best to have a good heart. It is free from wrong before God and before people."

Find It in the Bible
ACTS 24:1–16

PAUL SPEAKS TO FELIX
PART TWO

Paul continued telling his story to Governor Felix:

"I came to Jerusalem bringing gifts for the poor. I simply wanted to offer sacrifices. While I did this, they found me in the temple, and some Jews from Asia were there. They're the ones who should be here today. They may have something against me. These men here should tell you another story. I was brought to their council. There I mentioned that God would bring us back from death. Maybe that's their problem."

Felix knew quite a bit about the Christian way. "The Roman captain must come here," he said. "Then I'll decide this matter." Guarded by soldiers, Paul had the freedom to see his friends.

A few days later, Felix sent for him. The apostle explained the gospel to the governor and his wife. They heard about God's judgment. Self-control was a part of Paul's message to them. These and other things frightened Felix. "Go away for now," he told Paul. "I'll send for you again when I can." What he really wanted was payment to set Paul free. The apostle waited there for two years.

Find It in the Bible
ACTS 24:17–27

PAUL DODGES AN AMBUSH

A new governor named Festus came to power. As a favor to the Jews, he kept Paul in prison. In Jerusalem, the priests and leaders gave Festus a bad report about Paul. "Do us a favor," they said. "Send Paul here. We'll settle this problem." In fact, they planned to ambush Paul and kill him.

"No," replied Festus. "I'll be in Caesarea soon. You come down, and we'll settle this." In Caesarea, the Jews falsely charged Paul, but they lacked proof.

"I've done nothing against the Jewish law," Paul replied. "I didn't pollute the temple, and I always respect the Roman emperor."

Festus said, "Do you want to go to Jerusalem to settle this?"

"I've done no wrong to the Jews. You know this. I'm not trying to escape. But I've done nothing that deserves death. So no one can turn me over to them. Instead, I'll take my case to the emperor in Rome." Paul knew he'd be killed if he went back to Jerusalem.

Festus talked with his council. Then he said, "You want the emperor to hear your case. Therefore, you will go to Rome."

Find It in the Bible
Acts 24:27–25:12

THE KING HEARS THE GOSPEL
PART ONE

Agrippa, the king of Galilee, and his wife, Bernice, visited Festus in Caesarea. "I'd like to hear this man Paul myself," said Agrippa.

"Tomorrow," agreed Festus, "you'll hear him."

The next day, King Agrippa and Bernice were escorted by military leaders and city rulers. "King Agrippa," Festus announced, "here is the man I mentioned. People claim that he should die. But he has done no wrong."

The king spoke to Paul: "You have my permission to speak."

"I'm glad to tell you my story, King Agrippa," Paul began. "You know the Jewish customs and matters of their law. Please listen patiently. I'm on trial because I believe God's promise to our ancestors. All the Jews hope for this, as well. It is that God will bring us back from death. Yet now they accuse me because I believe this!

"I hated the name of Jesus. I was furious and punished Christians. I even traveled to faraway places to arrest them." Paul described what happened to him at Damascus. He told the king of his heavenly vision.

Find It in the Bible
ACTS 25:13–26:19

THE KING HEARS THE GOSPEL

PART TWO

Change your mind! Turn to God!' I declared this wherever I went. I told Jews and Gentiles. That's why the Jews tried to kill me. But God has helped me. My message is the same as Moses and the prophets: Christ would suffer; he would be first to return from death; he would give light to all people."

"You're out of your mind, Paul!" exclaimed Festus.

"This is the levelheaded truth," said Paul.

"Do you want me to be a Christian?" asked Agrippa.

"I want you all to be like me—except without these chains."

Find It in the Bible
ACTS 26:20–29

PAUL'S PERILOUS VOYAGE
PART ONE

T his man has done nothing wrong," the king said as he left. "He could have been set free. But now he has to take his case to the emperor."

Paul, Luke, and Aristarchus traveled to Rome with several other prisoners. They set sail with the Roman centurion, Julius, in charge.

From Caesarea, the ship sailed north along the coast of Judea. They anchored at Sidon. There Julius allowed Paul to visit his friends. The ship left the next day. It didn't land again until reaching Myra in Lycia. There the prisoners were moved to a ship from Alexandria. It was carrying wheat from Egypt to Italy.

Sailing was slow because the wind was blowing the wrong way. Finally, they came under the south side of the island of Crete. There they entered the port of Fair Havens. They had lost many days getting this far in the voyage. Winter would have to pass before they could sail on to Italy.

Paul spoke to the ship's captain and her owner: "I can see that this will be a dangerous voyage. The cargo will be lost, and so will our lives." But they paid no attention.

Find It in the Bible
ACTS 26:30–27:12

DAY 357
PAUL'S PERILOUS VOYAGE
PART TWO

air Havens wasn't a good place to spend the winter. "Let's take a chance and put out to sea," the captain said. "We'll try to reach Phoenix." This nearby harbor would be safe from the winter storms. They drew in the anchor and set sail close to shore. Soon a violent wind rushed down from Crete. The ship couldn't be turned to face the storm. The northeast wind drove them out to sea. Struggling for control, the crew lowered the sea anchor. The only sight was sea and sky. They were driven into the unknown.

Find It in the Bible
Acts 27:12–26

PAUL'S PERILOUS VOYAGE
PART THREE

The storm pounded violently. Soon the ship's tools, equipment, and cargo were tossed overboard. While the tempest raged, no one saw the sun or stars. All hope was lost.

Paul spoke to everyone: "Last night, an angel from my God stood by me. He said, 'Don't be afraid, Paul. You must speak to the emperor in Rome. God has granted safety to those who are sailing with you.' So keep up your courage. I have faith in God. It will be just as I've been told."

Fourteen days and nights the ship drifted across the Adriatic Sea. Then, at about midnight, the sailors guessed that they were near land. Testing the water's depth, they saw it was getting shallow. "We'll run onto the rocks!" they cried. Four anchors were dropped from the stern of the ship. They prayed for daylight.

In the darkness, the sailors tried to leave the doomed ship. Paul told Julius the centurion, "These men must stay in the ship. If not, no one will be saved." The soldiers made sure the sailors stayed.

Find It in the Bible
ACTS 27:18–32

SHIPWRECKED ON MALTA

It was just before dawn on the storm-tossed ship. "We've not eaten for two weeks," said Paul. "Please, have some food. It will help you to survive." Everyone watched Paul. He took bread, gave thanks to God, broke it, and began to eat. Then all 276 people in the ship took food. Everyone ate and was satisfied. Then they threw the wheat into the sea. This made the ship float higher in the water.

When daylight broke, they could see land. There was a bay with a beach. "Run the ship aground at that beach," ordered the captain. Anchors were cast off into the sea. Steering oars were untied, ready to use. The foresail was raised, and they made for the beach. But before the ship hit the sand, it struck an underwater reef. The vessel was stuck. Its stern, pounded by waves, broke up. Danger was all around.

The soldiers said, "Let's kill the prisoners or they'll escape." But Julius wanted to save Paul and wouldn't allow this.

"If you can swim, jump overboard!" ordered the captain. The others came ashore floating on pieces of the ship. Everyone was brought safely to land.

Find It in the Bible
Acts 27:33–44

PAUL ARRIVES IN ROME

Paul's ship wrecked on a little island named Malta. The kind natives built a fire for the cold, wet survivors. Paul brought some brushwood to the fire. Suddenly, a snake in the brushwood bit Paul. But he shook it off into the fire. They expected Paul to drop dead. Nothing happened. The superstitious natives thought this meant Paul was a god.

The father of a Maltese nobleman named Publius lay sick. Paul put his hands on the man and prayed. He was cured. All the people on the island then brought their sick to Paul. They also were cured.

Three months later, they set sail on a ship called the Twin Brothers. Sailing in front of a south wind, the apostle finally landed in Italy. Believers from Rome walked fifty miles down the Italian coast to greet Paul. He gratefully thanked God for them.

In Rome, Paul lived in his own house with a guard. The Jewish leaders visited Paul. "We've heard bad things about the Christians," they said. "But we'd like to know what you have to say." They set a day to meet with him.

Find It in the Bible
ACTS 28:1–23

DAY 361
SALVATION IS SENT TO THE GENTILES

Many Jewish leaders from Rome listened to Paul, morning to evening. By the day's end, they were arguing among themselves.

"The Holy Spirit was right," Paul said. "He said this to your ancestors: 'They'll listen but won't catch my meaning. They'll see but won't understand. Your words will do them no good. They won't use their eyes to look. They won't use their ears to hear. They won't understand with their minds, turn to me, and be healed.'

"So I want you to know this: God's salvation has been sent to the Gentiles. They'll listen."

Find It in the Bible
Acts 28:23–28

DAY 362
THE DEATH OF THE APOSTLE PAUL

Paul's accusers never came from Jerusalem to blame him in Rome, although he waited two years. He may have been in Spain when the city of Rome burned. It is sure that he continued traveling. Paul always cared lovingly for all the churches.

Paul visited Crete and left Titus there to help the believers. Then he went on to Miletus, where his friend, Trophimus, got sick. Paul also visited Timothy in Ephesus. On the way, he left his cloak and books in Troas. But soon he was arrested again.

Christians had been blamed for burning Rome. This may be why Paul was arrested the second time. God decided he would not be released. Instead, the apostle was convicted and beheaded by the Romans.

Before he died, Paul wrote to Timothy from prison: "It's now time for me to leave this life. I've fought a good fight. I've finished the race. I've kept the faith. The Lord has a crown waiting for me. He'll give it to me on the day he returns. Everyone who loves him and his return will get such a crown."

Find It in the Bible
ACTS 28:30; 2 TIMOTHY 4:6–8

DAY 363
JOHN'S VISION OF JESUS CHRIST
PART ONE

I was in spirit on the Lord's day." These words were written by the apostle John. He was a very old man. John continued, "Behind me, I heard a loud voice like a trumpet." John was in prison because he spoke God's word. His prison was on a lonely island called Patmos. He was the last of the disciples who had walked with Jesus.

"I turned to look when I heard the voice," John wrote. "There, walking among seven gold lampstands, was Jesus Christ." John had last seen Jesus sixty years before when Jesus came back from death.

Find It in the Bible
REVELATION 1:9–13

DAY 364
JOHN'S VISION OF JESUS CHRIST
PART TWO

John saw Jesus Christ walking among the lampstands. Christ was wearing a long robe with a golden sash across his chest. His hair was as white as snow. His eyes were like flaming fire. His feet shone like polished brass in a furnace. His voice was like the sound of many rushing streams of water.

John saw seven stars in Christ's right hand. Out of his mouth came a sharp sword. His face was like the sun shining with full force. "I fell at his feet," John said, "like I was dead. But his hand touched me. 'Don't be afraid,' Christ said. 'I'm the first and the last. I'm the living one. I was dead, and look, I am alive forever and ever.'

"Then Christ said to me, 'Write down what I'll show you. Send the book to the seven churches in Asia. These seven stars are the angels of the seven churches. These gold lampstands are the seven churches.' "

John wrote a great book called the book of Revelation. This book includes letters to the Christian churches. It also tells of the end of time. Finally, Revelation shows us what eternity with God is like.

Find It in the Bible
REVELATION 1:12–20

IN ETERNITY WITH GOD

I saw a new heaven and a new earth," John said. "The holy city, New Jerusalem, came from heaven like a bride dressed for her husband.

"A loud voice came from God's throne. The voice said, 'God's home is with humanity. He'll dwell with them; they'll be his people. God will wipe every tear from their eyes. Death will be no more. Grief, crying, and pain will be gone. Old things are passed away. I'm making everything new.'

"New Jerusalem has God's glory. It is green like jasper, clear as crystal. The twelve gates are named for Israel's twelve tribes. Each gate is a pearl. The twelve foundations are named for the Lamb's twelve apostles. These foundations are built of precious, colorful stones.

"Its one street is pure gold, transparent as glass. Out of God's throne flows the river of water of life. The tree of life grows on the river's banks. Its leaves heal the nations.

"Then Jesus said, 'The Spirit and the bride say come. Anyone who wishes may freely drink the water of life.' "

Find It in the Bible
REVELATION 21:1–22:21

NOTES

NOTES

NOTES

NOTES

NOTES

NOTES

NOTES

NOTES

NOTES

NOTES

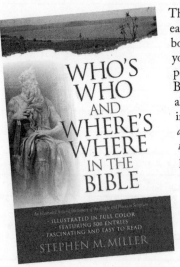